T0265611

This
MONSTROUS
Obsession

Hard Lessons Learned about Addiction

JAMES L. BAKER, M.D., M.P.H.

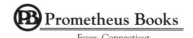 Prometheus Books

Essex, Connecticut

Prometheus Books

Published by Rowman & Littlefield
An imprint of The Rowman & Littlefield Publishing Group, Inc.
4501 Forbes Boulevard, Suite 200, Lanham, Maryland 20706
www.rowman.com

86-90 Paul Street, London EC2A 4NE, United Kingdom

British Library Cataloguing in Publication Information Available

Library of Congress Cataloging-in-Publication Data

Names: Baker, James L., 1952– author.
Title: This monstrous obsession : hard lessons learned about addiction / James L. Baker.
Description: Lanham, MD : Rowman & Littlefield, [2024] | Summary: "In his emotional, thorough, tender, and urgent new book, This Monstrous Obsession, James Baker, M.D., M.P.H., lays out the truths about addiction care that anyone with a loved one suffering from addiction must know. He writes not only as a veteran of hospice care and palliative medicine, but also as a parent who has lost a child to addiction"—Provided by publisher.
Identifiers: LCCN 2023041717 (print) | LCCN 2023041718 (ebook) | ISBN 9781633889446 (cloth ; alk. paper) | ISBN 9781633889453 (epub)
Subjects: LCSH: Baker, James L., 1952– | Parents of drug addicts—United States. | Drug addicts—Family relationships—United States. | Drug Addicts—Care—United States. | Drug addiction—Treatment—United States.
Classification: LCC HV5805 .B35 2024 (print) | LCC HV5805 (ebook) | DDC 616.86/03—dc23/eng/20231212
LC record available at https://lccn.loc.gov/2023041717
LC ebook record available at https://lccn.loc.gov/2023041718

For Macky

Contents

1

Risk

May 19, 2014, Holden, Massachusetts

"There's only one option left—but it's dangerous," said the Boston psychologist. He called himself an addiction specialist and had treated my son Macky, only twenty years old and already addicted to heroin for years. Terrified I would find Macky dead from an overdose, I was desperate for help.

Dangerous was exactly what I *didn't* want.

"What's that?" I asked.

"Give him two weeks to stop using," he said. "If he doesn't, then kick him out. Lock the door and don't look back. Don't hesitate or give him any more chances. That's it, there's nothing else you can do. He needs to know you are serious."

"But what will keep him from dying that night?" I asked.

He paused.

"That could happen. That's a decision you have to make."

* * *

I had already tried everything I could think of to help him. Counseling, emergency rooms (ERs), doctors, meetings, detox, rehab, even going cold turkey—an agonizing, archaic approach that worked in the movies but in real life was torture destined for failure.

Detox or rehab topped the list of what everyone told me Macky needed, and perhaps those options helped some people. Not Macky.

The detox center he agreed to go to in Worcester turned us away without even letting him get past the intake desk. We sat in a dirty lobby of a decrepit building that used to be a hospital but was bought by a national detox chain. They had put up some hopeful-sounding sign outside, but it still looked like the abandoned building it previously was, located in a run-down part of Worcester.

We pressed a buzzer, and a woman came out to the front desk, a beat-up bureau the buyers must have received when they bought the property, along with the other worn-out furniture in the lobby. The woman had me fill out some financial forms, and she took Macky's health insurance card. She went back inside while we sat in grimy chairs and waited for an hour. Macky didn't want to be there, but I had pleaded with him to try and he did it for me. I wanted him to get a "fresh start," like their advertisements promised.

The woman came back out and signaled me over.

"We can't help him," she said. "Sorry."

She handed me back his insurance card.

"But he really wants to stop. He's ready—that's why we came here. He'll cooperate," I said. "I'll help, too. Just let me know what I should do."

"We're not taking him. He's not in withdrawal, and that's what we treat here."

"Withdrawal? That will happen pretty soon. I've seen him like that before, and it's awful," I said. "Do we have to wait for *that*?"

"I'm sorry, sir, but this a detox center. Do you know what that means? You can bring him back when he's sick."

"Then what? What if I bring him back sick?"

"We'll treat him for three days and he can go home. Like I said, it's detox."

"Three days? What happens after that? What will you do for him?"

"Nothing. That's up to you and him. We'll wish him luck," she said with a straight face.

We got back in the car and started home. I said, "Goddamn it, Macky, what the fuck are these places for?"

"Making money," he said. "Why do you think they ran my insurance card instead of checking on me? They don't care what happens to the patients. I told you about these places."

* * *

I was a physician, trained in pain and palliative care at a prestigious medical school in Boston, but I knew nothing about addiction treatment. I had never had a single day of education about addiction care in all my years of training. Not through four years of medical school, three years of residency training, or my fellowship year in pain and palliative care. I never heard a single lecture about addiction where I trained in epidemiology and received my master of public health degree in Baltimore. Instead of discussing addiction and overdose, which was already killing tens of thousands of young Americans every year, I learned about things like diarrhea from tainted egg salad.

Addiction medicine wasn't even recognized as a medical specialty back then. There were more than nine thousand accredited training programs for other medical specialties but only a tiny handful of fledgling programs that taught anything about addiction. Not one program was offered accreditation. There were more than a million doctors in America at that time, but I couldn't find *one* to help Macky. I wondered how other families could find help when faced with the same plight.

I was just as lost as any other parent of a son or daughter with heroin addiction—confused, lost, and frightened.

3

In desperation, I followed the advice I was given.

I told Macky he had two weeks to quit and if he didn't I would throw him out. I could tell he didn't believe me, and I wasn't so sure if I could do it. But he kept right on using and even seemed to get worse after my warning. He still disappeared at night and slept all day and let go of his last connections with me and the rest of our family. When the two weeks were up, I did my best to stay strong and accept I had to follow through with the plan. I went upstairs to get him out of bed.

I said, "Hey, Macky. It's time."

He looked puzzled as he woke up and rubbed his eyes. It was around two in the afternoon, morning for him, just a few days before his twenty-first birthday. He had been living at my house in the small town of Holden, Massachusetts, because his drums and band practice room were set up in my basement. Sometimes he stayed with his mother, Patty, my ex-wife who lived in Sterling, the next town over. At least, he told me he was there after he had been gone all night, and I believed him. Patty and I had split up in 1996 when Macky was three years old, and he had bounced back and forth between our houses during the protracted divorce. My conflict with Patty continued throughout Macky's childhood, and parental strife was the only thing he knew about marriage.

"Huh? Time for what?" he asked.

"I told you what I was going to do if you didn't stop using and now I'm doing it. You have to leave."

He looked at me in silence for a minute, then asked, "What do you mean, Dad? Leave? Where am I supposed to go?"

"I don't know. That's up to you—the Salvation Army, a shelter, or the street if you have to. You have to find a way to stay safe somehow until you figure things out. I had to live like that when I was a teenager and I survived. Now you'll have to figure something out, too. Maybe Mom will take you in. But you're leaving right now and we're not going to debate it."

He came downstairs wearing the same faded green sweatshirt and dark jeans he had slept in.

I said, "Macky, you need to take some things with you. It can get rough out there. I don't know what you want to take, but you need some clothes and some food. It's hard on the street."

He took a plastic grocery bag from a kitchen cabinet, went back to his room, then came back down with the rumpled bag half full. He slouched forward when we reached the back door together. He said, "You're really going to do this to me, Dad?"

"I have to, Macky. I'm not going to make it easy for you to just die in your room one day, and that's what's going to happen if you don't stop using. You'd better get a coat because it gets cold at night. I always hated being hungry, wet, or cold when I was on the street at your age. I'm not giving you any money because I know what you'd do with it. You can take your health insurance card with you—maybe that will help."

He took the card but didn't want the coat. He turned away from me and walked out the door. I snapped the deadbolt behind him, then locked the front door and all the windows and latched the cellar door. There were other times he had been locked out, like when I had to be gone for a few days and didn't want him and his friends in there while I was away. I could tell he had come into the house anyway by using a ladder to get up to a second-floor window. I had seen the ladder moved and footprints on the sill. I didn't want that to happen again.

I had a strange feeling, like I was watching a movie with some actor methodically throwing all those locks, forcing his son out. How cold, I thought. Who would do that?

But it was me, and the house became suddenly silent with Macky gone and possibly never coming back. There would be no creaking of the stairs leading to his room in the middle of the night, a sound that woke me up and left me feeling comforted that he was home.

Macky was now alone in the world with nothing but that plastic grocery bag with a few handfuls of whatever, some socks, and perhaps his "kit" of needles and spoons. He had no money and nowhere to go, and I was the one who did it to him. I couldn't shake the image of somber state police knocking on my door that night, asking softly if they could come in and talk to me.

* * *

I believed the Boston psychologist was probably right when he told me I had no other option but to lock Macky out. It was hard to understand, like the quote from an army major during the Vietnam War who said, "We had to destroy the village in order to save it."

I'm positive the psychologist was correct that throwing him out on the street was dangerous. It was only later that I discovered there were *much* better options, but I don't think he knew what they were and neither did I.

* * *

Macky had refused to go to any more rehabs after the one ghastly experience we had, and I had my own doubts about them anyway. I had heard over and over that "he needs to go to rehab," but I had also heard the term "in and out of rehab for years" because it rarely seemed to work. Advertisements for drug rehab were everywhere, with scenes of rolling hills covered in lush grass or overlooking beaches with sparkling blue water. The rehab industry enticed terrified parents who had enough money or health insurance to send their addicted kids to live in buildings that looked like Ivy League dorms perched on seaside overlooks or countryside hills. The pitch from the rehab owners was that somebody's child or spouse caught up in addiction would receive treatment, but the treatment—whatever it was—remained a secret. The ads usually showed smiling young people with clear, bright eyes who looked off into the distance toward some mystical future without drugs. To me, they looked more like Hollywood models instead of the thousands of people with drug addiction I had seen while working in ERs over the years.

Whether it was drugs or alcohol they couldn't stop using, the people with substance use disorders I saw in the ER were usually haggard, scarred, and bleary. Others kept their habit well-hidden and still went to work and raised families with nobody the wiser except for those of us who cared for them when a medical complication or overdose happened. Younger people with addiction who hadn't been in prison yet or repeatedly raped and had not yet been forced to live on the streets to beg or steal might have looked like anyone else their age except for their pinpoint pupils, needle track marks, and furtive glances for the exits when I cared for them.

I didn't have the money to pay for rehab stints in Malibu, California, or on "Rehab Row" in Delray Beach, Florida. Even if I thought these places could help Macky recover, I just couldn't afford the cost after my divorce. As a doctor, I could still get credit and borrow on credit cards for things I needed and occasional splurges on things for my children, but twenty-five thousand dollars a month for a rehab stay was far beyond my reach.

I had already lost my house and half of my retirement savings, but those rightfully went to Patty as she cared for our children. Our children shuffled back and forth between houses, and Patty deserved a home for herself and the kids, especially after all the sacrifices she made for all of us. She needed to put food on the table, keep the children dressed for school, and build something close to a stable life. She couldn't go out and work with four little kids at home. Everything else I had went to the lawyers.

Patty and I both thought the same thing about the kids' whereabouts. "If they're not here, they must be over there." As teenagers, all of them knew how to work that ignorant illusion and build secret lives.

I searched frantically for more money through using my maxed-out credit cards, shady lending companies, and my family in California. I had to meet my obligations for child support and alimony or face jail, but I still needed more—a lot more—to try to help Macky. I could only work so many ER shifts, pushing myself through evenings, nights, and weekends twelve hours at a time. Constantly sleep deprived, I had to figure out whether it was morning or night when my alarm went off at six. If I died of a heart attack from living like that, my family would have nothing.

After borrowing to the hilt, I looked for more money. One of the rehab advertisements I found suggested begging from strangers by creating a pitiable website, "borrowing" from funds I might have access to at work, or selling a grandparent's diamond earrings. "She won't even notice they're gone," the ad said.

I still spent money on musical equipment, though. I knew that was overreach, but playing together was how Macky and I stayed connected, and I wanted to cultivate that bond. My basement was set up with amplifiers, microphones, a full drum kit, cables, and electronic mixers. I even bought black lights and a strobe light for a Jimi Hendrix flavor. I wanted to be down there jamming with Macky or listening to his band pull a song together. At the time, I thought it was worth it. Still, everything I had spent on music equipment in my whole life wouldn't have paid for one month at a lavish drug rehab.

My divorce lawyer had a different understanding of drug rehab. He knew that the court would be aware of Macky's addiction and would want to know what I had done to get him into rehab. I told him that I didn't believe rehab would help Macky and that I couldn't afford it anyway. But my lawyer was in charge of how things were presented to the court and I had no say in the process.

One day in April 2012, I was at work when the law office called my cell phone. They said my attorney was on the line and needed to talk to me immediately. I said I was working and asked if we could talk later, but his voice bellowed through the line.

"I don't give a goddamn *where* you are—you get that kid into rehab today or the court is taking him away! You get me?" he said.

My attorney was six foot five and two hundred and fifty pounds with a loud, intimidating voice. That was probably why he won so many cases and the reason I was referred to him. I didn't expect him to treat his own clients the same way, but he did whatever was necessary to build his cases. Memories of my own childhood left me fearful of big, aggressive men, and my lawyer's approach triggered the same fears I used to feel. I acquiesced.

"Okay," I said. "I'll do it."

"Get him there *today* and make sure you can prove it," he said, then hung up.

I called Anne, my wife since I remarried in 2007, and told her what we had to do.

She never anticipated any of this drama when she left her quiet life in a quirky house she rented on Nantucket. She had started living there right after she finished college, waitressing and cleaning houses for wealthy renters in the summer. She later became a successful real estate broker. I was drawn to her remarkable dignity and kindness along with her emerald-green eyes. I had grown up in the wild 1960s in California and never imagined that later I would be attracted to grace and character. I never knew why she left that uncomplicated life to come over to the mainland and marry me, a dad with four kids in the middle of a messy divorce. What I offered seemed like the polar opposite of her life on an idyllic island.

I told her what my divorce attorney said and asked her to pick Macky up from school that day. We agreed that she would tell him that he had to meet me for a medical appointment. She found him walking home and picked him up, then drove him to an ER in Framingham that was halfway between our house in Holden and where I worked in Boston.

I was there waiting for them when they arrived, still wearing my doctor clothes and ID badge. Macky realized what was happening and was furious he had been tricked and lied to. He was only seventeen and still respected me as his father, and it wasn't his style to confront Anne about anything. There was no way out and he knew it. We sat in the waiting room chairs for hours, with no food and no conversation. He had a thick book in his backpack, like always, and kept it in his lap so he wouldn't have to interact with us.

I registered him when we got there, and the receptionist became nicer when she found out I was a doctor and had been at one of the major Boston hospital ERs for years. Her attitude stiffened again when I told her I was there because my son was addicted to heroin and needed medical clearance to go to rehab.

"Oh," she said. "Have a seat and we'll call you."

Of all the reasons people went to an ER, seeking help for addiction drew the most scorn. Those charts were dropped to the bottom of the pile and the patients waited longer than anyone else. We hoped that the patients would just give up and leave without being seen or that someone on the next shift would have to deal with them.

We didn't leave, and we gritted out the wait until a nurse called us into a little triage booth and asked the usual questions. She told us to go back and sit down, then eventually someone opened a door and called out, "Maxwell?"

She told me to wait and she took Macky into the treatment area behind a locked electronic door. Anne had gone home by then and I was alone in the waiting room.

A different nurse took over the triage desk at shift change.

I told her I was a doctor waiting for my son and asked if I could please go back and see him. I wanted him to know I was still there and wouldn't leave him.

"You know you're not supposed to be back there," she said.

She pursed her lips and said, "Come with me."

We walked back to the treatment area and she brought me to a locked psychiatric room. I looked through the small, wire-reinforced window on the door and saw Macky. I tapped on the thick glass. He frowned and turned away from me, barefoot and naked except for the paper gown he had on, open in the back. I knew he couldn't hear me, but I said, "I love you."

* * *

Eventually, he was seen by a doctor for a cursory exam, the same type I used to perform for what's called "medical clearance" of patients who were there because of addiction. Emergency physicians checked to see if patients like Macky had some medical catastrophe unfolding, and that was easy. We didn't want to get blamed if they died at a detox center or wherever we sent them, like a rehab, psychiatric unit, or jail.

I remembered how much I resented seeing those patients while other people with *real* medical problems waited for me. Like every ER doctor, I knew how to treat a heroin overdose immediately. Anybody, doctor or not, could learn how to do that in an hour. If the patient wasn't already dead we could almost always resuscitate them. But then they were in florid opioid withdrawal, violently ill, and acutely agitated. They usually ripped out their IVs and left.

I imagined that the doctor who saw Macky thought about how much he'd rather take care of sick people instead of drug addicts. Like me, he probably never learned that opioid addiction is a treatable condition and that without treatment it's more deadly than most kinds of cancer.

By the time Macky's lab tests were done and they let him get dressed, it was after midnight. A nurse came out and gave me a handful of papers and directions to a rehab facility our insurance would cover. We set off in silence because Macky was fuming and wouldn't speak to me the whole way there. We arrived around three in the morning.

The rehab center was in the basement of an old stone house on a gravel road in the middle of nowhere. It looked like it had been abandoned or just given away. I thought we had the wrong address, but I saw dim light coming from small casement windows covered with iron bars. A dimly lit sign said "Entrance" with an arrow pointing to the back of the house, where moldy concrete stairs led down to the basement. The slimy steps led to a beat-up metal door with peeling green paint. It smelled dank, and cigarette butts littered the landing.

I rang a doorbell that clanged like an old school bell. A minute later, a voice crackled from a rusty speaker box.

"Can I help you?" a sleepy voice said.

"Um . . . is this the rehab? We just came from the hospital for admission."

"Yeah. Rehab. Just a minute."

On the other side of the door, we heard a heavy bar slide. The hinges creaked when the door opened, and we walked into a damp, dark cellar with a dim bulb hanging from the ceiling. An old, tired-looking attendant dressed in a dingy white uniform yawned as I handed him Macky's papers. He made me fill out more forms. They were about payment, not health. He looked at Macky and handed him a flimsy hospital gown and a plastic bag. He motioned Macky to go behind a dented aluminum frame with a stained cloth stretched over it.

He said, "Take off all your clothes and put this on. Put your stuff in that bag."

Macky stiffly did as he was told, then walked out from behind the screen and stood in his bare feet on the concrete floor. A skinny man with straggly hair, wearing the same kind of gown Macky had just put on, leaned against a wall and eyed Macky up and down.

I thought, "That's my son—he's seventeen. Quit fucking *leering* at him!" but I didn't say it.

The attendant handed me the plastic bag with Macky's clothes, then slouched back to the metal door with the bar. He looked at me and tilted his head, meaning "Get out."

I leaned close to Macky and whispered, "This doesn't look right. I don't like it—maybe we should just go. Let's get out of here."

"You don't know what I've had to get through already, Dad. I can make it through this, too," he said, his face glum.

I went up the stairs to my car as the door closed behind me. I sat alone in the moonlight with the bag of Macky's clothes in my lap. I brought it to my face and smelled it. I thought, "What am I doing?" then got out of the car and went back and pushed the doorbell again.

The attendant knew who it was.

"What do you want now?" he said gruffly.

"I need to talk to you, please."

He opened the door and glared at me. I told him I was taking Macky home.

"You *can't*. He's ours now," he said. "You signed him in."

"Well, he's a minor and I changed my mind. I'm signing him out."

He looked ready to fight so I tried to stay calm. I wasn't going to get into a fistfight down there. I apologized for waking everybody up but told him I needed to take Macky home first and would bring him back later.

I didn't want to involve the cops in the middle of the night, but he must have known I would if I had to. He tore up the papers and handed them back. I gave Macky his clothes, he got dressed, and we left. The door slammed hard behind us.

"I told you that's what these rehabs are like, Dad," he said as we pulled away. We never talked about it again.

My lawyer demanded proof of the ER visit and the referral to rehab, but I didn't tell him what happened there. He had told me to take Macky to rehab and I did—that's all he needed to know.

* * *

That was in 2012, and two more years of heroin addiction followed. I wondered if I had done the right thing by taking him out of that rehab. I kept trying to help him by going to meetings and seminars together and sometimes separately. The meetings didn't seem to help any more than the first times we tried.

I found snippets of what Macky wrote in journaling he did. The flavor of his writing varied wildly with his state of mind—harsh and vulgar when he was using or elegant when he was sober. In one, Macky wrote about what he had said during one of his Alcoholics Anonymous (AA) meetings in 2013.

"There must have been at least two dozen bleary eyed men and women staring up at me, the shifty-eyed nervous wreck, preparing to deliver his 'story.' The rest of the crowd smoked and thought about how

they were going to score whatever it was they needed after the meeting. The hall had a pungent, almost gagging smell and blue hazy fog from so many cigarettes burning away in ashtrays."

He told the story of a sloppy overdose he experienced after shooting up in the parking lot of a drugstore near our house. He shared how he had vomited all over himself, with "puke running down my fucking Tommy Hilfiger shirt," and how he lied to the EMTs and told them he took too much blood pressure medication. He revealed how he totaled another car but weaseled his way out of trouble because neither the cops nor the ambulance wanted to deal with another smelly kid who had probably used dope but there wasn't any proof.

In an undated document I found later, Macky wrote about another one of his meetings.

"The AA crowd seemed to be losing interest. I kept droning on about bullshit that was really insignificant and just not nearly honest enough. They wanted to see humility. They wanted to hear the real awful shit that actually lands you in an AA meeting with a bunch of war-torn veteran drunks and drug addicts. Goddamn I was a fucking idiot back then. I just bullshit everything and spewed see-through lies. My dwindling audience was visibly disgusted and maybe just a little tiny bit delighted at what they were hearing, with my 'Sharing' and 'Opening up.'"

* * *

It wasn't until May 19, 2014, when I had had enough and followed the psychologist's advice. I locked Macky out of our house and forced him onto the streets in a last-ditch effort to make him stop using. I tried to break off contact with him and wouldn't answer his calls or letters—but at least those things told me he was still alive. I couldn't resist certain letters, though.

There was an e-mail from him sent on May 27, 2014, just eight days after I had locked him out. Whatever he was going to say, I was too jaded by then to believe him, but when I saw the first line I decided to read it anyway.

Dear Father:
Once again, I very much appreciate your concern and support. Of course I have not been clean and sober for very long at this point, and it is obviously not all fun and games; however, I believe my attitude is changing dramatically for the better. I realized long ago that the stuff would end my life, prevent me from achieving my goals and realizing my dreams, hold me back in every regard, keep me from having serious relationships and a family, and everything else that matters in life. I knew this while I was living that life, yet it did not stop me. Now I truly believe that I can have all of those things and that I <u>will</u> have them, if I just abstain from that one monstrous obsession.

Thank you again Dad,
With love—
Your son

2

Genesis

WHILE MACKY WAS GROWING UP, I DIDN'T RECOGNIZE HOW THE events in his life might lead to drug use or addiction. As a doctor and a medical scientist I never researched the causes of heroin addiction or any other kind of substance use, not even alcohol. If I had put aside my own issues and tried to understand my children I might have seen the flood of factors in Macky's life that pushed him directly down a path into drug use.

When nearly everyone around me tried to tell me what was happening and why, I wouldn't listen. I saw myself as an educated physician and scientist who knew better than everybody else. I ignored advice, even from professionals—especially if they criticized *me* or how I raised my children.

* * *

Macky's risk started before he was even born. I had read that genetics was a powerful risk factor for both addiction and alcoholism, but that sounded implausible to me. I thought those conclusions came from junk science, the kind with no validation or proof. I studied genetics in medical school, and from what I remembered, genetics determined hair, eye, and skin color and other physical traits in offspring. Genetics was also known to cause certain diseases, like sickle cell anemia, Down syndrome, and many other maladies. I refused to believe that anything in DNA from my parents determined my *behavior*.

I obviously knew that grizzly bears kill to protect their cubs and that birds fly south for the winter. Salmon swim upstream and flop their way over dams to return to where they were born, then spawn and die. Horses are bred for personality and temperament. I didn't believe that applied to humans because I thought we choose our own actions and determine our own fate. I also didn't want to believe that genetics determined human behavior because my own father was a brutal alcoholic, violent and vicious. Nobody was going to convince me that I inherited his personality. But I *did* drink alcohol, especially in the military and later in college—enough to get drunk and behave poorly. I didn't like being like that and permanently quit a long time ago. I never considered whether I inherited an alcohol gene, if there even were such a thing. But science said *yes*. Macky inherited it, too, from both his mother and me.

She and I drank a lot when we first started dating and continued after we got married. She stopped when she was pregnant or breastfeeding but then picked up again. We lived that way for years. Her father drank a lot, but he was a World War II combat veteran and I didn't judge the drinking that followed his service.

I never thought that any of my children were at risk because of my drinking. But a mountain of reliable science says otherwise. The strongest predictor of a child developing a substance use disorder—drug addiction or alcoholism—is *genetics*. That's why Macky's risk of drug use started nine months before he was born.

* * *

The next most powerful predictor of addiction is *adverse childhood experience*, when a child suffers abuse of any kind—physical, sexual, psychological, emotional—*any* kind of abuse. I didn't think that I abused

Macky at all and thought instead that I protected him the best I could. I never hurt him physically and it was unthinkable that I would ever sexually violate him. But in retrospect, my behavior inflicted psychological and emotional harm, and that's what abuse does.

Macky's genetic predisposition for substance use, coupled with the severe harm he endured as a young child, laid the groundwork for his later addiction. Many other factors contributed to what happened to him, and I thought through what those were. I eventually realized that *nothing* about his addiction was a "choice."

* * *

For Macky, the most significant issue I didn't resolve was the intense marital strife between his mother and me.

Patty and I had stopped getting along more than a year before Macky was born and we had decided to divorce. We stayed together while we figured out what to do. More accurately, we *fought* about what to do. Living in the same house with our relationship held together by a thread, we still slept in the same bed and were intimate when we weren't fighting. Patty became pregnant again, and on May 23, 1993, Macky was born.

Our fighting peaked around that time, with three young kids and then another baby. The major issue was our different approach to raising our children. I wanted them to have freedom and happiness, and she wanted rules and discipline, and we wouldn't compromise. The children witnessed our shouting matches and the constant, simmering bitterness between us. If Macky remembered anything from his first three years, it would be the ferocious battles I had with Patty that escalated through the years. All the kids probably grew up thinking that's the way parents interact, with unbridled verbal assaults every day. Patty and I didn't offer each other forgiveness, understanding, patience, or compassion.

The kids also watched both of us drinking almost every night because we made no effort to hide it. The only times I stayed away from it were when I had to work that night. On holidays, at parties, during concerts, going out for dinner, or even watching sports on TV, we drank more. Alcohol must have looked to the kids like a necessary part of having fun or enjoying life. They didn't know about our hangovers, compromised judgment, and sloppy behaviors. All four of our children started their lives with two parents who fought every day and drank almost every night.

* * *

I knew I couldn't live like that permanently and would have to get out of that marriage.

But even the thought of leaving my kids was devastating and I couldn't make myself do it. Nevertheless, as our relationship continued to fall apart I decided it was time to go. That was in 1996, and Macky was still in a crib. I convinced myself that if I left and started a new home, one that was peaceful and calm, the kids could be happy at least half the time. Without me around fighting with their mother they wouldn't have to cope with that ugliness in her house, either. I thought that leaving was the right thing to do even though it was going to be hard on all of us for a while. I didn't explain anything to the kids and barely said good-bye to Patty. I told her I was sorry but I had to go. I told her she could keep everything we had, but I couldn't live with her anymore.

She was gentle when I told her.

"Are you sure?" she asked.

The kids were upstairs asleep and I had not told them I was leaving.

"No," I said. "I'm not sure it's right. It feels awful. But I can't go on like this."

I walked down the driveway to my car, taking nothing as I left. I didn't know where I would go or what I was going to do. That walk down the driveway after the kids were tucked in bed hurt more than anything I'd ever done.

Whoever woke up first the next day must have said, "Where's Daddy?"

I don't know what she told them, but over time they learned the hard way that Daddy was gone and not coming back.

* * *

I thought Patty and I were done fighting after I left, and we needed to figure out an amicable divorce, if we could. That didn't happen. Our continued arguing exploded into a ferocious battle where nothing was out of bounds. We attacked and hurt one another through our lawyers, our friends and family—and especially our children. The kids were caught in the middle and became messengers of vile exchanges while they listened to vicious accusations. There was nothing they could do to stop it. Patty and I knew that the most effective way to torment or manipulate one another was to use the children. Each of the kids were victims, but Macky took it the worst.

The happiest part of his day had always been when I came home from work and then when we cuddled up reading before I put him in his crib. He also loved being in my lap in the early morning, just him and his blankie, while I read the paper and held him. When that suddenly stopped, he couldn't understand what happened. At three, he certainly had no concept of "divorce" and must have thought each new day that I would come home. I pictured him looking out the window perched on the couch and up on his knees waiting for me.

Things turned far worse quickly. Patty had a friend move in with her just days after I left. I hadn't known about their involvement until he moved in and started living with her. Our relationship had been deteriorating for a long time so I couldn't blame her—I had a friend, too. I started staying with her before long. That left the children with another man in their home, where I had been there as their father only a week earlier. After that, they had to cope with the fact that I was living with another woman instead of their mother.

I had no control of when I could see the kids, and at first I had nowhere to take them other than a donut shop or McDonald's. I didn't wait long before I introduced them to my new girlfriend. We set up quilts and pillows on her floor when my guys came over for an overnight. She was kind and caring to my kids, but the situation was awkward and uncomfortable for everybody, including *her* children.

When I drove the kids back to Patty's, Macky tried to pull me by the hand to the house.

"Come on, Daddy. You can come home. It's okay," he would say. "*Please*, Daddy?"

I had to leave him rolled up in a ball and crying as Patty carried him in.

* * *

There were times that the fighting became so heated that the police got involved. All the kids witnessed the surreal sight of black and white patrol cars racing up to their house with sirens wailing. Patty and I had been screaming at each other in the driveway, and somebody called the cops. We weren't physically violent and nobody got arrested, but the scene of me arguing in the street with uniformed police had to horrify my children.

By then our fights revolved around the children's visitation schedule. And money.

We never resolved our differences and kept up our expensive, exhausting conflict throughout our children's lives, even into their adulthood. The turmoil was relentless and had to be excruciating to them. I should have realized what might happen to my children if they ever discovered that alcohol or drugs would ease their minds, even if that relief were only transient.

* * *

I thought I would have a settled place to live with my children in months, but it took me years. By then, the children had changed. They were still the same kids I knew and loved, but they had started to come into their own.

The three older ones shined in different ways, in academics, athletics, and social connections—but not Macky, who lived in their shadow. He had trouble learning to read and struggled at school. There were times when my daughter Cuff, my oldest child, or my sons, Casey and Homer, tried to help Macky with schoolwork, but he became so frustrated that he just gave up and dropped his head on the papers in front of him and cried. Nobody was a showoff, but Macky still felt inferior. He became quiet and isolated from everybody—except Homer, whom Macky always clung to.

None of the kids knew which parent they would be with on any given day because I had a different schedule in the ER every month. Even after it came out the schedule changed as shifts were moved around or traded at the last minute. Cuff, Casey, and Homer all had friends they could lean on, but Macky was increasingly unsettled and troubled. Nothing was going right in his life—not in his home, with his family, or at school.

* * *

Suddenly, letters on a page made sense to Macky, and he could read.

Go, Dog, Go! was his first book.

He went through a slew of children's books rapidly. As he continued on in grade school, he enjoyed chapter books. Before he started high school, Macky discovered classic literature, including ancient Greek works and more modern literature—and the edgier the book, the more he liked it. Noir became a favorite genre, dark and frightening fiction that I never liked but he loved.

He also discovered books from the Beat Generation, in which jazz music, counterculture, and drugs were glamorized, particularly heroin. Macky seemed seduced by the concept of a cloistered community of intelligent, rebellious outcasts who made their own rules.

He put together the drum set I bought years before and started to teach himself to play at age eight. He practiced constantly, and by the time he was ten or eleven he put a band together. I tried to teach him rock and he went along with the three-chord songs I knew from my era, but he worked much harder on learning avant-garde rhythms. He loved listening to old-school jazz musicians and was entranced by the way those musicians lived their lives on the edge. Macky even took saxophone lessons with a fantasy that he could be the next John Coltrane, but after a few months he realized the sax wasn't going to be his instrument.

Writing songs and playing in his band became an obsession to Macky. He studied the lives of his favorites, going back to Gene Krupa and Buddy Rich. He knew drugs were often part of the music world and I think he imagined that life as a musician living on the margins might be right for him. His heroes had been shunned by society but found each other and made their own way.

The movie *Pulp Fiction* came out when Macky was eleven, and by the time he was thirteen he watched the video. I saw it with him a couple of times and watched him lean forward when heroin was cooked, drawn into a syringe, and injected. He was mesmerized by that scene and I was disturbed by his fascination.

* * *

Alcohol seemed to dominate advertising, especially during the sporting events we watched together on TV. The commercials showed people having fun, flirting, and celebrating, alcohol being the most important element needed for pleasure and enjoyment. That bothered me because of all the alcohol-related illness and death I had seen in the ER, things like cirrhosis, pancreatitis, and seizures. I could also smell the metabolites of alcohol in the blood dripping from car accident victims. Macky never knew that side of drinking and instead saw the sexual allure that advertisers had actors portray.

I didn't know if the empty liquor bottles I found hidden in the back of a closet in 2006 or buried underneath trash at the bottom of a garbage can in 2007 were from my kids, a girlfriend or boyfriend, or just their friends from school. I wasn't as strict about it as maybe I should have been. Like a lot of people back then, I thought "at least they're at home" instead of out in a car.

* * *

Even though Macky made progress and showed joy through his music, the pleasure of discussing literature, and playing with his brothers and me in the backyard, he had an undercurrent of gloom.

When his darkest troubles emerged I took him to a child psychologist. The doctor saw right away the primary cause of Macky's sadness and anxiety.

"Jim, do you see what's happening with Macky? Do you know why he's struggling?" he asked.

"His mother won't listen to me. I'm trying to help him and she undermines everything I do. She argues at every turn and Macky's the one who suffers. That's the problem," I said.

"You're right about *one* thing—you two are causing his symptoms."

"So you agree. How do I make her stop?" I asked.

"No, I don't agree. It's not 'her' that's the problem. You're *both* hurting him. If you don't stop, it will be permanent."

"Doctor, I'm not doing anything wrong. You should see what it's like dealing with her. This is not my fault."

"Listen to me. You *and* your ex are ruining Macky's life."

I glared at him.

"If you don't stop, this will come back to haunt you. You're putting him in danger," he said.

During more legal battling with Patty in 2009, the court ordered an evaluation by a guardian ad litem, an independent professional to represent the children. She performed an exhaustive evaluation and reached the same conclusion as Macky's psychologist: that the problem was *both* parents' behavior. I tore up my copy of her report. The judge knew better and issued orders for Patty and me to *stop* our conflict or the children could be taken away. My own attorney told me if I didn't pull myself together one of the kids might later wind up in prison or dead.

The same child psychologist saw one of my other boys, also caught in the middle. He asked the doctor what to do the next time he felt caught in the middle of a fight between Patty and me.

"Tell them to go fuck themselves," he said.

* * *

Despite all the complex challenges in Macky's childhood, he also found meaning and fulfillment at times.

26

All the kids went to summer camp in Sterling, where they learned to swim in Lake Washacum and formed teams with other boys to compete against each other in whatever games the camp counselors organized. One of those competitions was called Capture the Flag, which I knew nothing about except that they all loved it. Macky found himself a leader on his team, maybe because he was finally among kids his own age instead of his bigger, faster brothers.

One summer, we decided to skip that camp because we had so many other things going on, and by then Macky wanted to focus more on his music. We were at my house when I got a call from someone at the camp. He asked if he could talk to Macky. They spoke for a few minutes, and when they were done Macky went upstairs and retrieved the clothes he had worn at camp the year before.

"Hey, Dad. I need a ride to the lake. Can you take me?"

"For camp? I thought you were done with that."

"They need me. The kids can't play Capture the Flag because they won't listen and nobody can lead them. I've got to get down there. Let's go."

He grabbed a towel, his water bottle, and some snacks from the cupboard, then threw them in his backpack and stood by the door waiting.

He wasn't giddy or playful. This was serious business to him, and he needed to go take charge.

* * *

Macky saw both of his older brothers win first-place trophies when each competed in their different age-groups in the kiddie "tractor pull" at our town fair. The boys pedaled a tricycle towing a concrete block on a conveyor belt. The yearly contest was a race to see which boy was the toughest and most determined.

Macky had never defeated anyone in a contest of strength, but he was old enough to enter that race and fight his way forward. He pedaled with all he had and won. He held his trophy tightly, exhilarated to be just as strong, capable, and respected as Casey and Homer.

* * *

Macky also found niche subjects where he could be the smart one. He taught himself geography, and at the dinner table he quizzed his brothers about obscure countries around the world. He learned the history of continental drift and how geology proved how that happened. The other boys gave him credit but still weren't very impressed and said, "So what?" But I felt happy that Macky could have his place in the sun.

After that, he became interested in biology. My friend Eric had majored in bio in college and enjoyed teaching Macky about trees, plants, microorganisms, and cells. Macky especially liked knowing about mitochondria, the tiny organelles that generate power within cells. For reasons I never understood, he always wanted to know about the smallest components of everything.

Neuroscience really captivated him. He started with learning which areas of the brain controlled things like motor function, vision, memory, or emotions. He learned that synapses, the tiniest spaces between nerve cells in the brain, were critical to how all brain function was coordinated. Macky steered conversation to the things he knew and relished, finally achieving a place at the top of the family totem pole, at least in scientific knowledge.

* * *

Macky's small successes in science, literature, and music helped to build his self-esteem, and my marriage to Anne in 2007 seemed to bring him a sense of consistency and predictability. She made rules the best she could as a stepmother, and by the time Macky finished middle school in June 2008 he knew he had dinnertimes, responsibilities around the house, and accountability. I thought he was going to recover from all the hardships he had faced as a young boy and would overcome his emotional difficulties just in time for high school.

Maybe he would have continued his remarkable growth and development, but by summer, living in a new home in a different town and suddenly separated from his friends, his troubles emerged again.

He had a genetic predisposition toward substance use and had suffered emotional abuse from my years of combativeness with Patty while we used him as a weapon to hurt one another. I wouldn't listen to his teachers, his psychologist, or anyone else about the damage we were doing. He had already started drinking and was in a precarious state by the time he started high school.

But then something beyond our control unfolded and placed Macky's life in a new kind of danger, along with an untold number of other Americans suffering from emotional or physical pain. The prescription pill epidemic arrived.

* * *

A major change in American society had swelled from an early threat in the 1990s into a terrifying catastrophe within another decade. Purdue Pharmaceuticals discovered the enormous riches they could acquire by manipulating gullible doctors into prescribing their blockbuster new drug OxyContin. Together with distribution companies and pharmacies, they manipulated the Food and

Drug Administration, evaded detection by the Drug Enforcement Agency, and proceeded to seduce physicians into pushing these addictive pills onto the public. They did whatever they could to coax physicians into collusion. Money and sexual favors were the most effective methods. Purdue also persuaded otherwise reasonable physicians to prescribe their drugs by providing what they called "education." They paid respected academic physicians to lecture community doctors about OxyContin and convince them that this powerful opioid was safe and nonaddictive.

Neighborhoods across the country suddenly had medicine cabinets stocked with opioids, the worst of which was OxyContin. Before long, millions of addictive pills pervaded every community, including rural towns like Sterling and Holden.

Macky had money because I gave it to him—I didn't want him to experience the poverty and hunger I knew growing up. He had his computer and his cell phone and knew how to use them far better than I did. He had privacy in his basement apartment to do whatever he wanted without supervision and a ready excuse to be almost anywhere at any time because Patty and I didn't communicate and he knew it. He had unrestricted access to the whole world through the internet, and I never monitored what he did.

Macky had major risk factors for addiction, along with money and around-the-clock internet access. Patty and I still failed to work together. I felt overwhelming guilt about what was happening. Maybe every parent feels the same way at times. Addiction specialists later told me, "Jim, this is not your fault." I hope other parents hear that message, too.

Still, by the end of the summer of 2008, Macky was on the edge of disaster.

3

Deception

Excerpt from an essay by Maxwell Baker, 2013:
"I started with, you know, cheap painkillers like all the other spoiled, stupid rich kids like me. Then it became something else as it, well, as it always does, right? Then bam! I'd wake up in CVS parking lots with my automatic in reverse and my foot on the brake. I'd shot up in CVS and Walgreen's parking lots quite a bit . . . and at red lights. Anyway I'd gotten high and then pulled out of the space immediately to get the fuck out of there. I'd driven in reverse about twenty feet before my lights went out. When the EMTs and a cop were shouting at me through my rolled-down window, I dreamt that I was far away from that lot and driving south towards Grafton. Then I finally heard their distant weirdly echoing voices. It felt like I was underwater, swimming at a public pool and everyone above the surface was yelling about something urgent. Eventually, my eyes started blinking open, and I felt that woozy numbness of an almost lethal overdose."

* * *

Although he didn't start using pills until he was fourteen or fifteen, Macky started experimenting with alcohol in 2003, when he was ten years old. Both my house and Patty's had liquor around, and the kids could get to it anytime they wanted to. Many years later, an older friend of Macky's admitted he was the one who introduced Macky to drinking. He said they chose vodka because they could replace what they drank with water so the bottle didn't look tampered with.

I never thought I needed to worry about Macky drinking in the fourth grade, but I didn't know what he did when he wasn't with me. I had left Patty in 1996, when he was three years old.

I didn't think any of the kids drank, especially Macky because he was just too young. He must have been suffering more than I realized and searching for relief in any way he could find it. He couldn't have known that those choices might ruin his life.

* * *

I didn't know when Macky started smoking pot, but it was probably around 2005, when he was twelve. That's when he went on vacations with Patty and the other kids every summer, always to the same place. Those times were special for all the kids and their mom to be together and frolicking with the other families on vacation in Maine. For a couple of weeks every year they were free from the conflict that always simmered back home. I didn't ask about who was there or what they did because Patty and I were already divorced and her time with the kids was none of my business.

As my kids stayed out at night with other kids on vacation they must have experimented with a lot of things, especially if they behaved like I did at that age.

* * *

I rented a house on the outskirts of Sterling in 2001 and lived there for seven years. The house was on a country road with thick woods just beyond the backyard, with ponds and a reservoir back there somewhere. Deer, packs of coyotes, and moose wandered into our yard, and I'm sure bears quietly sniffed around at night.

The boys were there with me a lot, and they made the most of the big yard and long driveway, playing football, baseball, and other sports all the time. I gave them the freedom to do almost anything they liked and trusted them to be responsible. They had friends come over every day, and that's when Macky invited his first musician friends over and started his band.

Late one night, I checked around the house to see what everyone was doing. Macky was inside with a friend playing a computer game, but the older guys were outside. I went out and smelled marijuana among a huddle of the older boys gathered together out in the street. I brought my guys inside and talked to them about the dangers of drug use and maybe getting arrested. I could see that my lecture about "danger" didn't convince them. I had already told them about my wild life in the 1960s, and I couldn't take that back.

* * *

All the kids went back and forth between Patty's house and mine and made their own decisions about where they wanted to be. Sometimes I came home from work and found them alone at my house because they just took the bus there after school. I was comfortable that they could get something to eat on their own and do their homework or play on the computer if I wasn't there. They could have gotten into trouble, but I didn't suspect anything.

One thing caught me off guard. Sometime in 2004, a woman I had hired to help watch the kids and keep the house clean came downstairs carrying about half a dozen empty quart-sized liquor bottles. She found them in the back of a closet and put them on the table in front of me without saying a word. They weren't mine, and only the kids and I lived there, so at least one of them was drinking—a lot. Maybe all of them were, but I didn't know.

I had to face the fact that my children—at least some of them—were drinking and experimenting with drugs at my house, but I didn't know which ones were doing what. I wasn't alarmed because I remembered my own behavior at that age, along with most of the other kids I grew up with in California. My children must have been experimenting at Patty's house, too, and she probably didn't know about it anymore than I did.

They learned to say, "I'm going to Mom's," and I wouldn't question them. I'm sure they told her the same thing about seeing me. They knew that my refusal to communicate with Patty enabled them to go anywhere they wanted without explaining a thing.

That freedom led to a big problem on Memorial Day weekend of 2008. Macky turned fifteen on Friday, May 23, and he had planned a party for the whole weekend. Patty thought he was going to be with me and I thought he was going to be with her, so we were both gone.

On Saturday, I got a call from the mother of one of Macky's friends.

"Do you know where Macky is right now?" she asked.

"Yes. He's at his mother's. He went there for his birthday and he's spending the weekend. Is there something wrong?"

She was furious. "He's drunk!" she said. "I'm at the house right now and nobody's here except a bunch of kids and they're all drinking. Who's supposed to be *watching* them?"

She had called her son, one of Macky's school pals, to check in with him and discovered something was wrong. She went over to Patty's and found out what was going on. At first, I was fuming with intense anger at Patty for leaving him alone, but later on I had to admit that there was no way she could have known where Macky really was because I refused to communicate with her. Once again, it was my children who paid the price for our behavior, and as time went on the consequences were increasingly dangerous. Macky had just turned fifteen and was partying with other adolescents, drunk and on drugs, with neither Patty nor me aware of what he was doing right in his own home with a manicured lawn in the suburbs. If a police car had driven by, how could the officer have had any clue what was going on inside?

That scary event was partly my fault because when I dropped Macky off at Patty's I could tell nobody was home and I still left for the weekend. He had told me he was going to be with her and I believed him, thinking she was just out for a while and would be back soon. I preferred dropping him off when she wasn't home because I didn't want her to come out and start asking me questions that usually escalated into another stupid fight.

I had come back to town as soon as I could after I got that call from the outraged mom who discovered the drinking party, but the damage was done and none of the other parents trusted me anymore. When I picked him up and confronted him he owned up to what he did—and for reasons I never understood he also chose that time to tell me that they were smoking pot, too.

His life of finding peace through substance use was now out in the open, but I had no idea how bad it was about to become.

* * *

The drinking party was in May, and in July we moved to a huge home that Anne and I bought in Holden. The house had a really nice spacious, finished basement with a bedroom and a bathroom. All the doors down there had locks.

The basement was the only area in the house where Macky could set up his drums and play hard whenever he wanted, so that's where he went. Macky also put my amplifiers and other equipment down there, so his bandmates could just show up with their guitars and maybe a favorite amp and start playing. Suddenly our house became the primary hangout for Macky and his friends. I knew the back door might be a problem because it led straight to the backyard and a path through the trees leading to the street. Nobody could see from inside the house who came or went through that door, day or night.

We had just moved from Sterling, the tiny town where Macky lived his entire life. He left the only elementary school and middle school he ever attended and was about to start high school at a giant regional school where he hardly knew anybody. His sister, Cuff, had moved away for college. His brothers were in the upper grades at high school by then and had cars, girlfriends, and after-school jobs. Over a few months, the bandmates came over less and less often because it was hard on their parents to bring them back and forth. The guys drifted away, and Macky found himself separated from his family and friends. I felt sad for his loneliness and isolation. He longed for the closeness of his brothers, but they were growing up fast and had other things to do.

* * *

High school started for Macky in September 2008. Suddenly, he was among thousands of students instead of the small group of friends he had at the elementary school in Sterling. He was still barely fifteen and unsettled by the crowds of bigger, stronger, older kids who were all strangers to him. At graduation from middle school, he was looked up to as the "smart guy" and a leader. At the high school, he felt like a guppy, a nobody in the eyes of those eighteen-year-old seniors with grown-up bodies, cars, and confidence.

At his new regional high school, even lunchtime was no longer a cherished break to hang out with his friends and maybe learn to flirt. There, lunchtime was divided into four different blocks and the students rotated through the different time periods every few weeks. The daily gathering Macky had known for the past eight years changed into a rapid-fire feeding time, like at a zoo.

He no longer had teachers who knew him well and had time to focus on how he was doing or know if something was troubling him. At the high school, class sizes were much larger and class times ticked by in forty minutes or so before the bell rang. The students scurried to their next classes to avoid tardy slips and detention. I witnessed the pandemonium whenever I went there to meet with teachers or attend school events.

The teachers layered on reams of homework because they had so little time to teach in class. My other kids had spent hours every night trying to keep up with the burden, but Macky resisted the drudgery of what he felt was rote memorization. He did the minimum to get by without getting in trouble. Instead, he practiced his drums, wrote, and read long books—just not the ones they assigned. He couldn't stand high school and disconnected early on.

One morning in his first month there, Anne came to me and said she was worried.

"I found alcohol in Macky's backpack this morning. I thought you should know."

"What? How did you find that? What were you doing searching his backpack?"

"I wasn't 'searching' it. I put in his lunch and saw a bottle of mouthwash that looked brown. I opened it and it was whiskey."

"Anne, that's his most personal stuff. Every kid in high school tries drinking. Also, Macky's struggling there—he's just trying to escape. Please don't go through his things."

* * *

37

Macky didn't want to get up for school and started going in late. He told me that there was an administrative day or that he didn't have first period—anything that could delay his having to go. But then I got notices from the school about his tardies and absences. I asked him about it and he said he was sorry, he must have made a mistake.

He started to wear the same clothes two or three days in a row and stopped fixing his hair the way he used to. Lunches came home uneaten. I asked about his homework, and he told me he finished it at the library. I didn't believe all these suspicious things he told me, but I thought he was just overwhelmed and would adjust to the rigors with a little more time.

New musicians started coming over, always through the back door. I heard them playing and went down to listen, then found older kids I'd never seen before. Some of them were talented players, but so many cycled in and out that I got to know only one or two.

Some of these guys had the bleary-eyed look and thick speech of the drug users I'd seen so often in the ER. They showed me what seemed like fake respect just so I wouldn't throw them out.

"Nice to meet you, Mr. Baker. Nice place. Thanks a lot for having us here," then they'd look away and play a chord.

Later on, I asked Macky, "Where are you meeting these people? Are they from school?"

"Nobody at school can play. I find them online or at open-mic sessions at clubs."

"Clubs? What does that mean? You're not old enough to get in."

"I get in as a performer."

"What do you know about these guys? They're in my house, Macky, and there are things here I don't want anybody touching."

"It's my house too, Dad."

As the school year continued, I went to PTA meetings. Nearly every one of his teachers told me Macky was not doing his work. They said he was capable but didn't seem to care. Several asked if there were problems at home.

"Yes. There's a divorce, we recently moved to a different house, and his brothers aren't around anymore. He's having a really hard time dealing with everything all at once."

The high school offered to help and connected Macky with their genuinely caring, concerned guidance counselor, but no matter how nice she was, Macky still wouldn't listen to her.

* * *

He had been ordering drum parts online, and I had given him my credit card. I thought his focus on music would bring up his mood, which had turned surly. But when more and more packages arrived I thought he didn't need *that* many drum parts. I opened one that felt squishy. Inside was a big bag of what looked like pot. I showed it to him and asked what was going on.

"That? It's 'spice.' It's like fake weed. It doesn't even do anything, and it's legal," he said. He leveled his eyes at me and said, "Why did you open my mail?"

"Hey, I need to know what's going on. I squeezed that package and knew something was wrong."

"Yeah. Thanks a lot for respecting my privacy," he said and slammed the door.

I knew he kept on ordering things because I saw the charges on my card. I didn't know where all the things he bought were being delivered because he knew I was watching and was cagey about whatever he was up to. When another package came to our house, I opened that one, too. Inside was a sealed bag with a stick-on label saying "Bath Salts."

I thought, "Macky takes bubble baths? I can get that at CVS." I realized later how asinine that assumption was, but that's what I thought in the moment.

By the end of his freshman year in 2009, Macky was in bad shape. He slept in every day, then bashed his drums for a while and slipped out the back door. The band could still play, but their music was sloppy. I packed up their stuff to drive them to a gig one night and found one of the players on all fours on my front lawn throwing up. I was disgusted by how these guys behaved, especially right before a big performance, but I was glad that Macky still focused on getting the show put together even though he wasn't really doing well, either. "At least he's not out on the front lawn throwing up," I thought.

* * *

Even though our relationship had become more distant, we still talked. He knew I was a pain doctor and wanted to know about the strongest drugs I prescribed.

"Do you use Opana?" he asked.

"What's that?"

"You don't know Opana?"

"No. I don't know every drug there is."

I had to look it up to learn that it was an expensive, ultrapowerful prescription opioid that caused so much addiction and death that it had to be taken off the market. He asked about other opioids, too, and knew a lot about what was out there. I thought that either he was curious about what opioids I had to use to treat my patients or that his friends were using them. I didn't want him in that crowd, but music had become the center of his life and I didn't want to interfere.

* * *

By 2010, a cascade of events unfolded that should have knocked me to into awareness like a baseball bat to the face. Everybody in Macky's life insisted that Macky was using drugs and that I had to help him. I refused to believe them and felt people were ganging up on him right when he needed support instead of judgment. I fought back with a vengeance.

When suspicious events started to happen, I came up with an explanation for all of them even if my excuses made no sense to the people around me, including my family. Money disappeared from my wallet and Anne's purse, enough to make us start hiding them. My bank called me and said someone tried to cash one of my checks, but they could tell the signature wasn't mine. I knew the teller after years of banking there and asked her if it was Macky, and she said no, it was someone his age she had never seen before. I blamed one of his new friends and told her it wasn't necessary when she offered to show me the bank video recording. I didn't care who it was as long as it wasn't Macky.

A parent called me and said they found one of my prescription pads in their son's backpack. I wondered how their son got into my locked home office and into my desk. My briefcase had been rifled and foreign banknotes with big numbers but no value were gone.

When I went to the pharmacy, I asked if Macky needed anything. He wanted Q-Tips and alcohol swabs. When I asked why, he told me needed them to clean his ears.

"You need a whole box of Q-Tips for your ears?"

"I clean my drum equipment, too."

He crashed his car late one night and said he fell asleep after work. He either quit or got fired from every job he could find, including at a car wash. He spent hours in my garage, and at first I thought he was cleaning it but then found a typewriter, candle, and burned matches on a plate by a window on the upper level. I thought he wanted to be a writer and he was creating his fantasy version of a writer's loft, and I was happy to imagine him as a young Hemingway.

Anne asked me about things she thought were missing from the garage, like some of my power tools. I told her to stop being nosy. "I know what you're thinking, Anne, and I don't like it," I said.

He lost his phone, then his keys.

Then one day he told me that a friend of his suddenly died the night before. I knew him, a soft-spoken, friendly guy.

"*What?* How did that happen?"

"Hard to believe, Dad. He overdosed. I just saw him the other day and forgot my phone when I left. I went back over to get it today and there were cars everywhere. I knocked on the door, and when somebody let me in to get my phone, I asked what was going on and they said, 'You didn't hear what happened? He died from an overdose.' Heavy."

* * *

Patty wrote to me and said Macky was using drugs. Anne told me. His friends' parents told me. My brother in California was incredulous.

"Jim, he's using drugs. You don't see that?"

"I told you, it's those fucking guys he's hanging out with now. I can see it a mile away," I said. "One of them was barfing in my front yard, someone stole my checkbook, and now money goes missing. I don't know how to get him away from these people."

He started wearing long sleeves every day, then a dark sweat-shirt, then a hoodie. He *looked* like a heroin user, but I thought he liked the outsider, tough-guy look. His eyes were droopy, and he seemed half-asleep at the dinner table. I asked him about it, and he said he had allergies and had to take Benadryl. I told him there were better choices I could recommend.

His nose was runny when he emerged from his room with a constant sniffle. I asked why he was like that so often. He glared at me.

"I told you I have allergies. Now I have a cold. You're a doctor. Why are you hassling me for being sick?"

"Sorry, man," I said. "Just want to make sure you're okay."

Things got even worse, but I was intransigent. By then, the people closest to me were insisting that Macky was using drugs and that I had to accept it to help him.

"I *know* about addiction," I said. "I've seen thousands of people with addiction in the ER and resuscitated so many that I can't even remember them all. Hundreds, maybe a *thousand*. You think I don't know what drug addiction looks like? I grew up in Los Angeles, and I survived living on the streets in San Francisco right after the Haight-Ashbury thing. I played in bands most of my life and half of the musicians were on something. A guy overdosed and died when we were classmates in *eighth grade*. Heroin was everywhere in Vietnam when I was there—half my unit came up positive when they did a surprise urine test. I saw it every single day. Nobody's going to tell me I don't know addiction when I see it."

Maybe I really could detect drug addiction in people—but not in Macky.

* * *

He dropped out of school and was either asleep all day or up all night, or had gone off somewhere without even telling me he was leaving.

Then I found a syringe under his bed, the needle caked in dried blood.

My hands trembled when I showed him what I found.

"That? Dad, that's from Steve, the guitarist who stayed over last Friday. He's a diabetic. I can't believe he left that in my room. Sorry."

I breathed a big sigh of relief.

I heard something rattling in the dryer and found a butane lighter. I told him the house could have burned down and asked why he carried a lighter if he didn't smoke. He told me his friends smoked.

I found blood-tinged alcohol swabs in his bathroom trash and asked about them.

"You're going through my *trash* now?" he barked.

"No, Macky, I'm not 'going through your trash.' I saw bloody gauze in there when I emptied the bathroom wastebasket. I thought maybe you had a bleeding problem."

"I cut myself shaving."

I opened his top dresser drawer to put his clean socks in and saw little baggies with white dust in them. More white streaks were on the dark felt on the bottom of the drawer.

"Those goddamn guys are using *right in his room* now?" I thought as I put his socks in and closed the drawer.

* * *

My understanding of Macky's problem changed one night in a heartbeat.

It was the fall of 2010, with the leaves already down. Anne had made a big supper and finished all the cleanup. We got the living room fireplace going. Anne put her feet up on the couch and settled in to read, with the house finally quiet.

Within seconds, the band room directly below us lit up with a powerful blast of sound that shook the furniture. Anne was stunned at first but then realized what was happening. She rolled her eyes back and put her hand to her forehead.

I noticed immediately how together they were, starting from the first beat. They continued on with clean changes and perfect balance. Anne and I looked at each other. She was exasperated, but I had to suppress a satisfied smile about how good they sounded. I loved having a live rock concert right in my living room. After a few songs, they took a long break. I guessed they went outside because they didn't come upstairs and I thought I heard the heavy basement door shudder against the wall when it closed.

They came back in and I could hear the amps hum again as they powered up. Macky pounded a few beats on his amplified kick drum and then did a few snare rolls. I was looking forward to what was next.

As soon as they started the next song, everything was different. They couldn't get the intro right and Macky's beat was off. I couldn't believe how awful they sounded as they tried to find a rhythm. Anne gave me a quizzical look and lifted up her palms.

"What happened?" she asked.

I knew what the problem was immediately and felt sick to my stomach. I had played in enough bands over the years to know when there was friction between the players, someone was drunk, or someone had a fight with a girlfriend and couldn't focus. This was different. This was the sound of heroin.

Heroin use was the worst thing that ever happened in any band I played in. Whenever someone used, they didn't care how they sounded anymore and couldn't pull it together no matter how much they tried. And that's what I heard that night—from the drums. Macky's command of the band's dynamic rhythm disappeared during that break.

"Were they drinking?" Anne asked.

"No," I said as it all became clear to me. "That's either heroin or some other kind of serious dope. And Macky's the one who's doing it."

I was stupefied by how blind I had been and how I had fought with everybody who had tried to tell me the obvious truth.

Other things came to mind—the loose brick in the wall behind the drum set that could be pulled out to reveal a secret space, like in a prison cell; the acoustic tiles above Macky's bathroom that I saw had been moved to create hidden shelves above the tiles; and the times when Patty had texted, over and over again, "Was Macky with you last night?" I had ignored her because it was my pattern to brush off every communication from her. I also didn't want her to know that he often *wasn't* with me the night before and I had no idea where he was.

All the pieces fit together and suddenly made sense. Macky had deceived me to protect himself, but I also deceived myself and refused to see what he had been doing for nearly a year.

It was as though the monolithic dam of denial I had built inside myself had suddenly burst.

4

Addiction

Essay written by Maxwell Baker for college English class, March 2014, "Scrambled Eggs":

In the bus station downtown, I get the needle in easily enough without a tourniquet. Blood shoots softly in a thin cord into the barrel of the syringe. I close my eyes and wait for the rush. I feel it first in my face and hands. That pins-and-needles sensation washes over me, and I forget everything else. It's almost too intense. There is always a bit of fear with a powerful shot. As the drugs race through your veins and the feeling builds, you're never quite sure if it's going to put your lights out.

I usually fill the syringe so there's just a little room to pull the plunger back. If you have the patience and the discipline, you push the plunger real slow, and when it's halfway depressed, you wait for the rush and then finish the shot. That way you don't inject it all in half a second and send a bunch of heroin and cut straight to your heart. It's extremely unpleasant when you get chest pains from shooting dope. Even worse than chest pains is shortness of breath. Every once in a while, I feel like I just can't get enough air.

The dope game is a dance where one false move means at the very least a near-death experience. It's very surreal. You think that because you have never had an overdose in however many years, it won't happen to you. But then someday, you shoot up, only to wake up twenty minutes later sitting on a toilet without having even wiped your ass and with no feeling in your legs. Even if you dodge that roller-coaster ride, it doesn't mean you won't nod off at the wheel and kill yourself, someone else, or both. It's pure luck, and all it takes is for that luck to run out once.

Heroin is the best and the worst drug. Sure, you might vomit twenty times in a day. It's not all that unpleasant, though; it certainly isn't like throwing up after drinking too much. Dope gives you energy, yet it calms you down. It gives you confidence but keeps you reserved. With the right dose, you can outdo any sober man when it comes to sex. If you can finish, it might take two hours or more just to get there. Nothing I can think of compares to the feeling you get immediately after ejaculating while heavily under the influence of opioids.

Don't let me fool you, though.

I absolutely would not recommend injecting heroin or any narcotic—ever. The first time you get the guts to try it, it's nerve-wracking to say the least. After that, all you can think is, "What's the big deal? I want another." The life of a junky, addict, user, whatever is dominated by incredible highs and desperate lows.

You find yourself doing things you never imagined doing. A rich white kid from the suburbs will catch a habit and end up on the street, selling everything he owns, stealing, and robbing just to get another shot.

You're sick more than you're high no matter what unless you're a gazillionaire. Even with a million dollars, you would be either out of cash in maybe a year or, much more likely, dead by the end of the first week.

Once you get a taste of it—and I don't mean smoking, snorting, or anything else other than intravenous use—that's it. You're never going to forget it. You may not become addicted, but you will absolutely not forget those first few moments of sheer bliss. It truly is a disease. For me, it took a very long time to admit that opioid addiction actually is a disease. It's something you catch that cannot be cured. If you get clean, you have to fight every single day to stay clean. Addiction will haunt you for your entire life.

If that is not enough, being high almost all the time and sick for the rest, you will become a robot. Your only function and most of your thoughts will revolve around dope: how to get it, how to pay for it, and how to get away with it. Dope robs you of your humanity.

Good powder smack, which is all I ever really do living in New England, is like a powerfully attractive and exquisitely beautiful woman. I mean not all the junk I do is good. It took me years to find that one connect. The holy grail of dealer. This is a guy who has a *constant* supply of consistent and very potent, properly cut heroin. He has layers of insulation. He (or even she for that matter) has drivers, dealers, etc. This guy is a consummate professional. He speaks Spanish, he speaks English, he knows what he is doing.

After a while, you pretty well learn the ropes of being an addict. I never sell dope. I won't kid myself and tell you it's because I don't want to ruin other people's lives. It's for the sole reason that an addict absolutely cannot possess heroin without doing all of it in short order.

Years of buying dope, shooting dope, and everything that goes along with it does teach you a few things. It teaches you that money isn't really worth much. Sure, money can buy you things like a house, food, and all kinds of stuff. What I mean is that dope teaches you that money is just paper. You will trade that paper away in a heart-beat. The money is worthless in a way; you don't want the money, you care only about the dope that the money can buy you. What I'm saying is you could have a whole lot of cash, but that cash isn't really worth anything because it will all end up going into your veins . . . catastrophically and irreversibly fucking up your life.

The insane world of dope teaches you other things also, lessons relevant to the sane and sober world. It teaches you how to live in some goddamn scary and dangerous places. It teaches you how to respect other people who are in the gutter because you've been there. It can teach you most importantly how beautiful and valuable life is. If you make it out of the hell of addiction and get sober, you begin to see that heaven really is on Earth. A longtime junky who's gotten clean can tell you how incredibly good it feels to be sober and healthy. Your health is something almost everyone takes completely for granted. Only once good health is gone and you're sick or dying do you fully appreciate what it means to be healthy.

Life has so much opportunity, so much bounty, and so much beauty for us to behold. If you can dodge the pitfalls of vice, then life is filled with possibilities.

Sick as a dog on a Monday morning, I have about twenty-seven cents in the pocket of my pants laying on the floor next to my mattress. It takes me a good twenty minutes to slide out of that warm bed. This time, there is no beautiful young girl whose name I don't even know pressed up against me.

I should just jump right out and get things moving. When you're dope sick, you're always cold. The idea is to do things as quickly as possible to avoid getting even sicker.

I yawn and get dressed. My eyes water uncontrollably, and my joints ache. The clock is ticking, and I'm not looking forward to bearing the freezing-cold morning when I go out to start the car up. My boots laced up, I stand and open the front door. Mother of God, it's colder than the coldest day in hell.

At least I've still got the old coupe. She always starts for me.

The car turns over, and the radio comes on playing some funk ballad by the Isley Brothers. I creep slowly over packed snow and ice, then down the driveway. After about ten minutes, I'm on the highway, and I realize I've left my only ticket to score at home. I scream some vulgarity at the jerks surrounding me in gridlock and try to move over to the exit.

Finally I'm back where I started. I grab the item I'll try pawning for the cash I need. Hopefully, the bastards will take it even though I've got a lot of stuff in there already. What is it to them? They'll probably more than triple their money.

Back on the road, I get that excited feeling that comes from knowing I'll soon have some heroin in my hands. It's enough to make me forget about being sick until I light a cigarette. Almost throwing up out my window, I gag and toss the butt. Sure I'd like that first morning smoke, but it won't come until the afternoon when I've got the drugs in me.

An hour later and I'm in the city. Not the one out where I'm living now, where a bunch of snobs go to get cut-to-shit wax paper stuff with stamps on it that say something like "Killer Queen," "Dead on Arrival," or "Just Do It."

I apologize to the guy in the tollbooth who lets me through even though I'm a dollar short. It's only a dollar, right? Wrong. I know this guy in the tollbooth. He's a fucking jerk-off who thinks he's a comedian and preys on poor fools like me.

I probably could get some high-quality gear back home, but I certainly do not have the money for that overpriced junk. Real heroin dealers don't waste their time; they know they'd still have customers if their product was just pulled out of someone's ass. More than likely, it was at some point. Actually, it was probably transported in someone's ass, only to be repackaged slightly and then placed in the runner or driver's mouth until he or she rubs off the spit and places the bag in your hand. The next leg of the bag's journey begins when you tuck it away in your sock, your mouth, or, if you're really paranoid, your ass. So all in all, this dope that I'd crawl through sewage and up out of a toilet to get to has by now been up two or more people's asses and in at least one person's mouth and touched by a countless number of grimy hands.

I'm in and out of the pawnbroker faster than expected, considering there was a guy arguing and trying to pawn a pogo stick or some equally ridiculous thing. Now I call the dealer for the second time, having given him about half an hour's notice. I can barely understand him on the phone, his speech is so slurred from benzos and methadone. I finally learn where I should go to meet him. The place is in a poor, crime-filled neighborhood where I won't have to remind myself of the switchblade clipped to my waistband.

I meet my dealer, Tim, and he promptly tells me the price has changed. I know he is a middleman, and it is by no means a secret. He claims to be very up front with me, saying things like, "Oh yeah, man, I only make ten bucks, you're lucky I even do it."

I know better than this, of course. In fact, he makes closer to thirty off of one bag.

I tell him that I'm short, that I have only fifty-five. Assuring me that it's not a big deal, I can just owe him, I promise to pay him in the next couple days. Luckily, this particular guy is in a deep benzo trance or fog in which he can remember almost nothing other than his own name. Two days from now, if he has a vague recollection of this transaction, it will seem like a dream.

Maybe he will tell me I still owe him after I neglect to pay. I have a good way of dealing with that, though, should it happen. A friend of mine, or acquaintance rather, is also a type of benzodiazepine robot. This guy may actually be worse, operating on some remote and very old portion of his brain. I'll tell the dealer that this friend of mine is the one who actually owes the money. This is perfect because neither of them can concretely remember anything. They will go back and forth arguing over things that may or may not have ever even happened. These kinds of heavily dependent benzo fiends are always sure that they are sharp as a tack . . . convincing themselves that they can only function when on copious amounts Xanax, Halcion, Valium, etc.

This is actually partially true. They simply cannot do anything productive when in withdrawal. When under the influence, in that impenetrable haze, they do manage to accomplish things, although it takes an inordinate amount of time. If I were to go into a grocery store, for instance, I'd get the groceries, pay, and get out. These guys work differently. In that grocery store, they might easily spend over an hour conspicuously stealing oranges or something before they remember why they were even there to begin with.

It often happens that a benzo fiend will go on a binge, eating pill after pill, until after committing numerous petty crimes, they wake up in a jail cell. Not being able to recollect what they did the night before or the whole week before, they vehemently deny that they did anything.

"No, I wasn't speeding and smoking crack with some kid that stole my wallet! I would never do that, man."

The risks one takes on benzos are insane. Your inhibitions are lowered significantly to the point where you simply cannot obey speed limits, stop signs, pedestrians, or other motorists.

Tim knows the city like the back of his hand, I'll give him that much, but it is the scariest ride I'll ever take on four wheels.

Sure, I might get to shoot my shot sooner this way, but I'm utterly convinced I'll either be killed or at least arrested on the way.

In no time, Tim and I pick up the stuff and get back to his parents' house. These parents of his are pretty lax. I mean Tim is twenty-seven and still living there. Luckily, they aren't home, and he lets me do my thing there. I go straight to the bathroom and get down to business.

A seasoned junky keeps his whole kit with him nearly all the time and definitely when he is going to pick up. The paraphernalia varies slightly among heroin addicts. They have either cigarettes, cotton balls, or Q-Tips for the filter. Most carry a knife, which is used mostly for cutting bags, filters, and what not. Syringes are "pins" or "rigs." The spoon comes in many forms. Some sleazy junkies skip cooking the junk, which, believe me, is very important. They just throw the gear right into a plastic bottle cap. Others like me use a thin metal spoon so the cook goes as fast as possible.

In the bathroom, it takes me about one minute to take the shot. I can do it at a long red light. I can get it done in a moving car. After hundreds or thousands of injections, an experienced junky can do it faster than a newbie can get it up his nose.

Sitting on the toilet, I wait for that old familiar feeling. The warm wave of euphoria referred to as the rush is always subtly different. This time, it comes on fast. Different batches of dope and other injectable formulations of opioids all take varying amounts of time to hit you, with the rush lasting different lengths of time as well. Oxycodone and pure morphine hit like lightning. Hydromorphone (or Dilaudid) and oxymorphone (or Opana) both produce an excellent rush and high. The oxymorphone is almost twice as powerful and gives a super clean rush and lengthy high. Typically, I avoid anything more potent than oxymorphone because the euphoria starts to drop off as the potency increases. Heroin, however, is the king of them all. If I'm ever able to acquire pure pharmaceutical heroin, I'll be in big trouble.

I clean the rig and leave the residue on the spoon, not wasting time to light up a cigarette. This first real cigarette of the day satisfies like you would not believe. Walking into Tim's living room, I see he's on the phone yelling at some guy who probably has very poor English. Tim calls him "Papi" and hangs up the phone after a couple minutes of frivolous conversation.

He asks me how the dope was. I tell him it wasn't bad but that I had to do the whole bag. He offers me a benzo so I might prolong the high and get a bit more out of it. Like always, I decline. Benzodiazepines work in conjunction with opioids, but personally, I can't stand them. The right amount, and you are still with it, but, as I have already made clear, benzodiazepines turn you into an incomprehensible zombie.

Not wanting to stick around Tim's so he can talk and talk and be my "pal," I ask him to take me back to my car. He says sure, but he needs another fifteen minutes or so.

"Ok, slick, I can live with that," he says. "Yeah, yeah. Yo, man—I was at the strip club last night, and I paid this girl to get me off, you know? Fucking amazing, bro. You ever gotten off with a Spanish babe?"

"Yeah once. I didn't have to pay her, though, Tim."

Tim starts talking about his girlfriend, saying, "Ahh fuck you, Max. Kim is so chubby now I can't even do her anymore. We're on methadone, and it fucks everything up. She's just . . . like . . . fat. . . . Then she's always begging me to buy hard. Like all that girl wants is fucking crack. I'm gonna dump her man . . . real soon."

Knowing that there's no way Tim will ever get rid of Kim, I almost laugh in his face. I'm always amused by his too-heavy Worcester accent, like "Bakah! What the fahhk, Brah. Pay me the fahk'n money already, kid!"

I go back to the bathroom to get anything that might be trapped in the damp cotton on the spoon and maybe even some powder left in the bag. I get a decent second shot this way, and now I'm content. The trick is to put out of your mind (as much as possible) the harsh reality that you are out of dope and that unless you score, you'll come down in a just a few short hours.

Tim finally gets off the couch and realizes simultaneously that he lost his keys. This is another reason I can't stand benzos. I lose my car keys, phone, and wallet enough as it is. I really cannot imagine having to deal with this kind of bullshit all the time day in and day out.

With the autumn sun setting fast, he starts up the car, and we fly to the supermarket parking lot, where I walk quickly to my car and get out of there.

A friend of mine lives about ten minutes away, and I call him up. I head over there and find Jake in his ten-by-ten tiny room. There's no paint on the walls, and the carpet is just something on the floor. Like always, Jake is sitting at a computer desk. The drawer of that desk is filled with about a hundred needles, empty bags, and spoons. He is sitting there chain-smoking cheap cigarettes and watching amateur porno. This isn't like him. He's not addicted to cocaine and pornography like Tim. He explains that this particular video features a girl he just met who left her cell phone at his house.

That is a major mistake there on her part, leaving her phone for Jake to peruse. She isn't bad looking. I think it's a common misconception that female heroin addicts are disgusting. She looks alright on the screen with a decent ass, nice breasts, and a cute face. I couldn't make it through more than half of her video, though; she is just not any good at what she's doing.

Jake the snake speaks for the first time in the five minutes I've been there.

"What's up man ... you get merked by Tim or what?" he asks.

I admit that I did. He surprises me by pulling out about two grams of good-looking dark brown dope piled on a book I gave him, *The Killer Inside Me*, by Jim Thompson. Even more surprising, he asks, "You want a line?"

I nod, saying, "You're not going to make me beg, huh?"

"You know I usually would but not today. I'm feeling generous."

"Thanks, man."

An hour later, I wake up in an uncomfortable wooden chair with drool on my shirt. The saliva on my shirt collar is better than the cigarette laying on Jake's lap that burned through his jeans. It's also better to have a butt burn through your pants than through your underwear. Before I nod out again, I hear footsteps coming down the hallway toward his room. I nudge him awake and motion to the cigarette butt balanced on his pants. He acknowledges it and puts it in a nearby ashtray.

Jake's neighbor and our mutual friend Charlie knocks on the door, saying, "Yo, you awake, dude? It's eight o'clock."

"Shit! I was supposed to meet my dad for a fucking seafood dinner," Jake says under his breath.

Jake unlocks the door and lets the kid in. He's all wired or maybe just normal, but we are so sedated he seems like he's flying. He tells us that we're "fucking idiots" but asks if we would like to jam. I agree, and Jake takes his time getting his Telecaster off the wall.

Charlie's got a cheap drum set, a few amps, a keyboard, and a PA in his basement, which is by all means good enough. I have my own sticks in my car to replace the toothpicks he has laying on the snare drum. I pull the snare out of the trunk and manage to carry the drum and some other gear in one trip. Jake dozes on a stool while I set up the kit.

Neither of these guys can truly play. Knowing chords and scales, having some theory knowledge, and being a decent reader doesn't make you a "player." I've been at this for over a decade. It takes thousands of hours pounding it out before you can be called good. It takes thousands more before you don't sound like anybody else and you've really got it. Playing with these guys isn't too bad. The hard part is playing with people who just can't play at all but think they can. It takes skill. If you're lucky enough to have serious, committed, and experienced musicians to play with, then things come together easily, although nailing songs perfectly is never a walk in the park.

By the time we're done, I'm soaking wet, and my ears are definitely ringing. Earplugs are a necessity when a drum set is involved and there is someone that knows how to use it, slamming down rimshot after rimshot. We chose to end it when, near the end of a song, the stick in my left hand shattered, sending a sharp piece of wood flying, like a throwing knife right by Charlie's face. It's funny, though: sometimes you get lucky and an ending like that actually works out with everyone finishing on the same note.

I climb the stairs with the boys and light a cigarette outside in Charlie's driveway. Charlie produces a marijuana cigarette and sets fire to that as well. I don't hesitate to partake, either. We go back to Jake's and shoot the shit for a while until Charlie gets a call from a high school girl and he quickly leaves.

Jake and I go back to his room and put on some music, I search my pockets for the fifteen bucks I neglected to give up to Tim earlier that afternoon. I ask Jake for a line in exchange for the cash. He gives it to me with a bit of reluctance. Not long after, I tell him I'm heading home.

Nobody's there when I get back. My brother is gone, and I've got the house to myself. I crack a beer and put a Steely Dan CD in the stereo. As soon as I get comfortable on the couch, I get a phone call. Having left the phone on the table in the kitchen, I wait a second before getting up and answering it. It's a number I don't recognize, but I answer anyway. This time, it doesn't pay off. It's a collection agency from Tulsa that reminds me of the three hundred six dollars and eighty-seven cents I owe Bank of America. Those pricks. I hang up and go back to the couch when the phone rings again. This time, it's a number I recognize alright.

"Hey, what's up you fuckin' queer?"

"Hey, asshole," I respond.

"You wanna chill, man?"

"Sure. I'm at my house."

I don't know if I'm up for hanging with him; he is my closest friend, though, there is no denying that. I microwave some pasta and turn on the tube. My team gets smoked as I catch the fourth quarter.

On the second floor is my brother's room, where he must have some hash or something. Sure enough, I find it right off the bat and borrow his glass pipe. I try to smoke it quickly on the porch so if he comes home, he won't realize I pinched some from his stash. Rick shows up as I'm getting it going.

"Always in the nick of time, huh?" I say.

"Ha! I know it's not even your shit, dude—let me in on some," he says.

"Okay, but remember, this isn't mine, my friend. This is some heavenly hash, though."

Dick Ryder tells me, "It's your lucky day."

I ask if he's got some dope for me on this Friday night.

"You bet your ass I've got some dope tonight. But do I have any for you? That depends."

"On what?"

"On whether or not you decide to leave my little sister alone. Don't take her out tomorrow night, and I'll split this gram with you."

"You've got a deal, pal."

A car pulls up in the driveway, and I grab the hash and the glass piece. I climb the stairs quickly and put the stuff back in my brother's sock drawer. I wash my hands and face, then come back downstairs as Jake, Charlie, and two teenage girls open the front door and step into my kitchen. One of the girls introduces herself as Genevieve. I can tell she isn't with either Charlie or Jake. The other girl, who is definitely good looking but less attractive than Genevieve, is introduced by Charlie as Jessica.

She interjects saying, "Just call me Jess."

"And you guys can just call me Gen," Jess's more beautiful female friend informs us.

"Okay, Genevieve and Jessica. That guy by the sink is Rick; he's a real jerk, so don't listen to anything he says. Right, Rick?" I said.

"Blow me, Max."

"See what I mean? Anyway, like he said, I'm Max. It's nice to meet you guys, I mean girls. Do either of you want something to drink? Vodka, beer, you name it."

Jess declines, but Genevieve says, "Yeah, do you know how to make a whiskey sour? Or if you don't, just a vodka and orange juice."

With a smile I say, "Sure, babe, anything you want. Big or small?"

She smiles back at me and indicates with a two-handed gesture that she would prefer it to be big.

I wink like a dumb kid and turn to make our drinks.

We go outside for cigarettes, and I give one to both girls.

Different cigarettes smoked on different occasions taste better or worse. On this warm night lit by a full red harvest moon, my Marlboros really hit the spot.

The six of us marvel at the sky and the huge moon until the color starts to fade from red to orange to golden yellow in just a few minutes. Having snapped a few photos, Charlie suggests that we go back inside and play some pool in the cellar.

"Not a bad idea buddy," I say. "Let's see what you've got. You wanna put some money on it?"

"Nah, bro. How 'bout this? If I win, then Gen takes her shirt off for us. If you win, then Jess gets naked. Sound fair, girls?"

Both of them gasp, then laugh, and, to my surprise, acquiesce.

Jake pulls open the slider, and we all head downstairs to the pool table. Rick switches on the lights, and I open up the fridge in the corner and grab a six-pack, handing them out and cracking one for myself. Charlie breaks, and we get the game going. I play to win even though I would love to see Gen in a little more intimate detail. Rick puts a David Bowie album on, and none of us can stand still except for Jake, who's nodding out on the sofa.

I say, "We'll have to do this again sometime with just slightly different rules . . . you know, higher stakes."

I find the Dire Straits record I'm looking for at the bottom of the stack. I put the needle down and stand up looking over at Gen, asking if she wants to have a smoke. Jake, Charlie, Rick, and Jess play doubles while I lead Gen up the stairs.

We chat while we smoke, and when I've finished mine, I say, "Alright, babe, I'm going to the bathroom. Give me a minute."

"Max, I know what you're going to do in there. Can I come?"

"Ahhh . . . woah, honey. What do you mean?"

"I mean I want to get down. Please?"

"You're sure? Well, okay, 'cause I'm not sure I know how to say no to you."

I ask her if she has ever done this before, and she says she has but only once. I ask her if she is absolutely sure she wants to do this, and she says, yes, she is.

I break out a small bump on a book and roll up a bill. She thanks me, takes the bill, and blows the line. I tell her I'll be right back, that it's something I'd rather not have her see me do. I shoot my shot in the bathroom. It only takes me a minute. When I come back to the room, I ask her, "How do you feel?"

She doesn't answer. She is lying supine on the bed. Those gorgeous lips of hers are now cold and blue.

5

Response

A COMBINATION OF COMPASSION, COOPERATION, AND COMPETENT medical treatment offers the best pathway for a family to protect the life of an addicted son or daughter. I didn't realize any of that when I discovered Macky's addiction. Instead I had contempt for his substance use disorder, distanced myself from his mother, and did not seek out medical professionals who knew how to treat addiction. Instead, my actions were driven by anger and fear, driven by my failure to understand *anything* about addiction—just like the rest of America, including doctors.

In retrospect, sometimes I fought for Macky with passion and determination. However, I often felt overwhelmed by the combination of my terror about the risks of his addiction, concerns about my own health, the evolving needs of my other children, and the complexities of balancing my new marriage and the demands of my work in medicine. While caught up in this whirlwind, I did not know how to direct my passion for Macky's survival in thoughtful, rational ways that would truly help him. That left me susceptible to believing almost any pitch about "recovery from addiction," even though almost everything I found cost more than I could ever afford.

I kept thinking about how my education and training as a physician did not include even the most basic teaching about the causes and treatment of addiction. How could it be that I had never received a single day of teaching about this disorder? My physician colleagues never received training about addiction, either, so how could they help? In the midst of the burgeoning opioid epidemic that gap in medical education was a recipe for disaster.

* * *

I was kind to Macky only in the very beginning, when I first realized he was addicted to heroin the night of the ruined band practice in November 2010. I believed he could just quit using and move on with his life the same day. In my mind, he could just stop the same way he chose to start.

I was determined to help and went to his room the next day to tell him I cared. I knocked lightly on his door in the morning, noon for him, then went into his bedroom. He was only half awake and didn't acknowledge me. His hair was splayed out on the pillow, and his knees were pulled up, rolling him into a little ball. I pulled the blankets up and smoothed his hair.

"Hey, Macky. Morning, buddy," I said. "We have to talk about something."

He didn't answer, but I saw him wriggle and knew he was listening.

"You're not in trouble, and I'm not mad at you. I love you, but I know what's been going on. I know you've been using heroin," I said. "Please don't try to deny it, and let's not get into a fight. I know a lot about drug use because of how I grew up.

It's hard to tell you this, but I know about heroin, too. When I was in Vietnam during the war all the guys I knew were on heroin, and it didn't take long for me to find out what it feels like, too. I was only in-country a few days and was in a sandbag hootch in the middle of the night. I heard the deep thunder from distant B-52 bomb runs and automatic weapons fire that sounded pretty close, but nobody seemed to care. They kept passing around what I thought were Southeast Asian joints, like Thai stick, but it wasn't. That's when I found out what heroin feels like and I'll never forget it. No wonder everybody got hooked on it. Please trust me that I know about drugs, including heroin. All I want to do is help you."

He was quiet for a moment and didn't open his eyes.

"I'm sure you do, Dad," he said. "But you don't know what it's like to be an addict."

He was right. I learned about the dreamy euphoria of heroin in a jungle hootch late at night in a combat zone, but I didn't understand the iron grip of addiction. I didn't know that shooting up heroin multiple times a day, every day, led to life dominated by finding the next fix.

For years, I had witnessed the dire existence of thousands of intravenous drug users coming and going through the ER every day, with severe medical complications or overdoses. I saw hundreds die. I thought they just wanted to get high, and just like in Vietnam, nobody seemed to care about the consequences.

"What are we going to do? How can I help you?" I asked.

"You don't need to do anything. I can stop. I've got it under control."

I believed him. I thought he could flush his drugs down the toilet, get rid of the needles, and start cleaning up his life. I had no clue there were changes in his brain brought about by his long-term addiction, with intense cravings he couldn't control and excruciating withdrawal if he tried to stop. He couldn't stop without medical help. Over time, receptors in his brain had been altered by addiction, but I didn't know that and neither did other doctors until much later, when sophisticated magnetic resonance imaging showed the drastic effects of addiction.

Macky could not return to normal the same day and go forward like nothing happened. I found out much later that the right medications could stop *withdrawal* symptoms fast, but the process of *recovery* from addiction and return to normal brain function takes years. My belief that he could turn off his addiction like a light switch was absurd, but at the time that's what I thought—anyone with addiction could stop whenever they wanted. My ill-informed, uneducated perception of addiction boiled down to my entrenched belief that addiction was a *choice*. To me, Macky had picked up a needle one day and all he had to do was put it back down. I didn't say it, but I thought, "Do you love me enough to stop?"

*　*　*

Even though I tried to be nice to him that day, I hated addiction and resented the people who suffered from it. During all my years in the ER, I saw what looked like a derelict habit that would go on permanently until the users were in prison or dead. They didn't seem to care what happened to them or what they did along the way. I had rejected early assertions that addiction is a disorder that could respond to the right treatment with support from family and community. Until recently, even the tiny handful of addiction specialists didn't have access to advanced brain imaging or know the biology of addiction.

Without appropriate medical care, people addicted to heroin will likely die—from an overdose or medical complications caused by daily injections of unknown concoctions sold on the street. They might be killed in a car accident, fall in front of a train, topple off a building, drown, or be murdered because of how they are forced to live. *Death* is the most likely outcome of heroin addiction unless there is treatment.

That's not how I understood addiction back then.

I kept thinking about all my years of education and training, learning about rare diseases or maladies with no cure, while we never learned about this treatable disorder, a condition that had already killed more than a million Americans in the past twenty years and would be on track to kill a million more in the next *ten* years.

I didn't see addiction as a health problem and wouldn't let go of my belief that addiction was a choice. To me, heroin addicts lied, cheated, stole, and committed crimes every day because getting high was the only thing that mattered to them. Maybe they would kill someone if they had to. They might kill *me* if they needed the money. I thought about the heroin addict who robbed me at gunpoint when I was eighteen, and I harbored contempt for people with addiction, not sympathy. My disdain for addiction clashed with my love for Macky, and I treated him with unpredictable swings that varied from gentle tenderness to vicious rage.

* * *

After countless overdose resuscitations in the ER, I knew what to expect when we injected Narcan into patients who had overdosed on heroin. As soon as the patients arrived, we put in a breathing tube if they weren't already dead. The nurses looked for a vein that wasn't scarred and withered by a thousand street injections, then tried to put in an IV. If they couldn't find one, I put a long needle into a central vein deep in the neck or groin. Security officers gathered around.

"Everybody ready?" I asked. "Okay, here we go. Narcan, two milligrams."

The patients usually started to come around—but not always.

"Two more," I said, as the doctor in charge.

In less than a minute, the patients shifted on the gurney, opened their eyes, and sucked in air. They yanked out the breathing tube, coughing, spitting, and moaning.

"What the fuck? Where am I? What happened?" they would ask.

"You're at the ER. You just overdosed."

By then, only a minute or two after the Narcan was injected, withdrawal set in and they sat up, dripping saliva or vomiting.

"Goddamn it, what'd you do *that* for?" was a typical question.

"Because you were dying."

"Just leave me the fuck alone," they might say as they pushed the nurses away and tussled with security.

They ripped out their IVs. Blood spattered around, and in our minds, it was probably infected with hepatitis or AIDS.

"Just let 'em go," I said. "It's not worth it."

They would stagger toward an exit and leave, a welcome sight to all of us.

"Probably going out to break into our cars now. Why do we even bother?"

I never offered anyone help after an overdose. We called someone with heroin addiction an "IVDA" in the medical record, short for "intravenous drug abuser." In the hallways at the hospital we called them far worse.

They often came in looking for prescriptions before states clamped down on giving out opioids. They would writhe around with fake back pain or migraine headaches or say they had a kidney stone—for that, they urinated into a bottle and secretly pricked a finger so there would be blood in their urine. We still knew. We called them "seekers" and sent them out with nothing. Fighting with them took more time than diagnosing a heart attack. We didn't recognize drug addiction as a medical problem and hated wasting precious time while the *real* patients waited.

My venomous attitude came out at Macky not long after we had that initial talk, when I told him how much I loved him and wanted to help. I found out he was still using after he told me he had it "under control."

* * *

I found out when I discovered he had pawned my guitar equipment.

I stomped into the Guitar Center in Natick, where he was working that day in the drum section.

"Hey, Dad!" he said as his face lit up with a surprised smile. "What's up?"

He didn't expect to see me walk in during the middle of the day.

"*This* is what's up!" I yelled. I slammed down a stack of pawn-shop receipts on the counter. "You stole my fucking amp and sold it for forty bucks? And my *bass*? You're that much of a goddamn *junky* that you steal from your own father?" I shouted.

I bared my teeth and leaned over the glass toward him.

He stood motionless and his smile vanished immediately. The paperwork in his hands drooped forward as he glanced around at the other employees and customers watching the scene unfold. He was cornered like an animal, helpless and afraid. Bits of saliva shot from my mouth as I blistered him with a relentless tirade, banging my fist on the glass between us, aware it might shatter.

I went on until my voice started to give out. I didn't care that his friends at work heard me call him a thief and a junky. My invective was so bizarre that I can't even remember what I said. I *wanted* him to feel humiliated. There was nothing he could do or say to stop me.

His eyes glistened.

As the store fell silent, I realized someone might call the police. I whirled on my heel and stormed out without looking back and didn't care what I had just done to him.

I had found those pawn slips when doing laundry earlier that day and found a little wad of papers in his jeans, and it took me a minute to realize they were receipts from a pawnshop in Worcester. I was puzzled at first but then saw the ones for my bass and amp. My initial confusion swirled into blind rage. I couldn't believe he would do that to me. He knew how I treasured my equipment. I loved to jam with my friends at night after work and cherished those times, and that was the same equipment I used when I taught Macky our first songs when he started playing his drums.

My heart pounded and my ears rang as I grabbed my keys to go confront him. When I got into the car, my hands squeezed the steering wheel and I banged on it at stoplights. I kept glancing down at the receipts next to me while my contempt accelerated the whole way there. I was in a frenzy by the time I got to him.

* * *

Later, I realized I had released the ugliest part of my personality on Macky, my youngest child, whom I had nurtured and loved his whole life. Maybe he *did* bring it on himself in some way because of his addiction, but I had overreacted in the extreme and inflicted emotional wounds that might not ever heal. I wouldn't be able to undo it later with "I'm sorry" or anything else I could say or do.

My anger was so intense and my behavior so vicious that I wondered if *I* had some kind of problem. That wasn't the first time I treated one of my children like that, and I had to consider if my outrageous actions might have contributed to his drug use in the first place. I also wondered if *other* families explode in anger when they discover addiction in a son or daughter, especially when the inevitable appalling behaviors that accompany addiction show up.

In retrospect, I should have realized that crushing his heart would steepen his downward spiral. It took me years to understand that cruelty and rejection would *not* help him recover. My actions made his problem worse. I should have known he would soothe his suffering by using more drugs.

* * *

My oldest brother, Bob, saw his son, Chris, become distant and troubled as a young teen back when we lived in Los Angeles. I saw it, too, and I remember Bob telling me, "That's just what they do at that age. It's part of growing up and he'll be fine."

Chris was warm and gentle every time I saw him, but he wasn't "fine" based on how he was doing in school. Bob was a cop on the dangerous streets of Compton for many years and then worked with the Drug Enforcement Administration investigating international heroin trafficking. Throughout his career, he had arrested young people for drug possession, informed families that their son or daughter overdosed, and handled countless crime scenes where victims had been robbed, beaten, or murdered in drug deals gone bad. Unlike me, he had sympathy for people who used drugs.

"They can't help it," he told me. "They're just trying to keep from getting dopesick. Dealers prey on them and they can't get out of it."

His awareness of the sorrows of heroin addiction didn't help him when he needed to find help for Chris, who became addicted as a teen. They got the same cold shoulder out there as they would have back here. Bob never gave up trying to help, which was particularly difficult in California, where their byzantine health care system placed addiction as their least concern. In Boston, we had much more sophisticated medical care—but the same disregard for addiction.

On one visit out there, Bob told me Chris had been shot but survived.

"He was just in the wrong place at the wrong time. It's rough out here."

I never learned any more details.

Eventually, Bob backed off on his police work to focus on helping Chris try to find recovery, then stopped altogether so he could help him get safely from one day to the next.

We both had careers where we came face-to-face with addiction but saw it through our different lenses—law enforcement for him, wearing a black uniform and carrying a gun, with me wearing a white coat and carrying a stethoscope. He was the one with compassion and understanding while I had bitterness and ignorance.

I thought he would be sympathetic to me when I was furious because Macky stole something again and lied about it. I wanted him to say that my anger was justified and that I was *right*.

"Jim, you know he can't help it, right? He's got a disorder called 'addiction,' and he can't stop it. He's doing what people with this problem do until they can find help," Bob said. "He's going to relapse, he's going to steal, and all those other things they do. He's only trying to avoid withdrawal—have you ever seen what *that's* like? He has a brain disorder and you need to learn that."

"Oh really?" I answered. "So it's okay for him to lie and steal because he has a 'brain disorder'? I should just let him do this to me every day, and that's just fine because 'he can't help it' because he has a disease? Like *cancer*?"

I was fuming.

"Jim, relax. Try to understand him. Macky can't change what's he's doing. He needs help," he said. "Do you know how to tell when an addict is lying?"

I was hopeful for a useful answer when I said, "No. Tell me."

"Their lips are moving."

Bob's calm, unruffled response to my fury made me hang up on him in disgust. I had refused to learn from his experience or listen to what he had to share. I turned against my own brother and did not speak to him for more than a year. Chris, Bob's only child, later died from an overdose.

* * *

My younger sister Judy, also in law enforcement in Los Angeles, was a DARE (Drug Awareness Resistance Education) officer for several years, trying to guide youth away from drugs. She and I wrote back and forth about Macky. As with my brother Bob, I wanted her to see how Macky's addiction was different. He was ruining my life, too. I had my medical career and three other children to raise, and I couldn't tolerate how Macky undermined my life and chose heroin over the well-being of his family.

She wrote back long, delicate letters. She shifted the focus to how I could *help* Macky instead of feeling sorry for myself—she told me the best approach was to gently guide him to treatment, care for him at home, and assure him I would always be there for him. I thought it was more of the same useless advice by someone who did not understand how hard my life was. I stopped speaking to her, too. Years later, she was promoted to commander in her agency. She sought grants and equipped thousands of her officers with Narcan and had them train in how to use it. She also worked to make Narcan available in the jails of Los Angeles and helped improve medical treatment for inmates with addiction. I don't know how many lives she helped save. She was *another* police officer who knew more about addiction than I did, but I still rejected everything she told me.

* * *

Anne tried to help me act rationally, but she, too, believed in compassion and the importance of structure and rules, so I fought her at every turn. I wanted her to be cruel like me and *brutalize* Macky into recovery. That was part of why we broke up and separated.

My other sons saw my anger and stayed silent about things they thought would set me off. When I didn't know where Macky was but they did, they told me he was fine—they couldn't take a chance on what I might do if I found him and whomever he was with.

Other parents and neighbors shared their concerns, but I accused *them* of causing Macky's addiction because he associated with their kids, some of whom used drugs. I refused to listen to their advice because Macky was my son and *I* knew him best.

I thought I could order Macky to pull himself together and stop because I gave orders in the ER, where they had to be followed. At home, though, I was powerless trying to order my children around. They humored me or ignored me, but they knew they rarely had to do what I said because I never established a structure of sensible, predictable discipline.

I wondered if other parents like me, in charge at work, thought they could also create rigid rules and a hierarchy at home. I thought they had no more control than I did if one of their kids had sex in middle school or started cutting themselves because they were depressed. I didn't even know that Macky created a secret life online, and I had no idea how to stop him even if I had discovered it.

When his drug use got worse I thought toughness and brutality would work, but all that did was push him away. During the handful of times when I listened to him and tried to understand his predicament, he showed signs of trust until I lost my composure again.

"I never know where you're coming from, Dad. I don't know when to believe you anymore—you tell me how much you 'care,' but then come in my room and attack me," he said. "It's different every day, and I don't know what to expect. It's like you're a different person every time."

"I'm the same person every time, Macky. I love you but *hate* what you're doing."

"You sure don't act like you love me."

"What do you want me to do? Tell you how much I love you stealing from me? Lying all the time? Being a *drug addict*?"

"See what I mean? That's just what I'm talking about."

* * *

Then I started drinking again. I didn't care what people thought about me because I was overwhelmed and thought nobody understood. When I drank enough, my self-control disintegrated and my behaviors changed from overbearing to outrageous. I wrote letters in that state, made stupid nighttime phone calls, and argued with friends and family.

When the alcohol took effect after a drink or two, I had a brief respite from how awful I felt, but when it wore off I felt even more isolated and sad. My boorish interactions and compromised judgment along the way damaged relationships and hurt the people around me.

I didn't hide my drinking from Macky and wondered if he thought, "Which one of us has a problem?"

He had to see that I was using a substance, too. I just used a bottle instead of a needle.

I stopped that self-destructive habit but not before I left people scarred from what I did.

* * *

I blamed Patty and she blamed me for Macky's addiction. Whoever's fault it may have been, that was the time to reach out to one another and try to help our son. Patty tried to get me to listen so we could help Macky, but I resisted and never consented to any plan she proposed. I stopped speaking to her even when I received her frightening calls or texts that she was terrified about what was happening. I didn't think we could ever work together and refused to cooperate. Macky knew that, and so did our other children.

* * *

I knew Narcan could reverse an opioid overdose almost immediately because I had administered it so many times, but I never tried to get some to have in the house. I should have offered it to Patty for her house and to Macky—and told him to never use alone because medical examiner records showed that most overdose victims died alone behind a closed door at home.

I didn't remove the bedroom and bathroom door locks, and I didn't know how to unlock the door from the outside with a bobby pin or a cheap tool from the hardware store. I didn't have a big hammer beside my bed in case I heard a thud in the night and suddenly needed to break a door down.

Macky carried his leather drumstick case with him everywhere, but I never looked for what might be in there besides drumsticks. Later, he carried a camera case with him all the time and told me he never knew when the right scene might appear. He had that camera case with him constantly, but I still didn't look for what else could be in that case. He was casual about it and I was in denial, so it was easy for him.

Homer's girlfriend, Lauren, asked, "Why does he always have that camera case with him? He even takes it to the *bathroom*."

"He probably doesn't want to lose it. He knows how valuable it is," I said.

The thought of what he might be doing with that never crossed my mind.

I didn't look in the glove compartment of his car, under the front seat, or in his trunk.

I tried to monitor where he was and when by putting a tracker on his phone. I think he discovered that right away, and soon I was tracking his *phone*, not him—he knew where to leave it. Then he reprogrammed it to spoof his location, and after that he removed it altogether.

I could have checked the history on his computer but didn't. He could have danced right around that through a virtual private network, back channel, or fake app, but I still wish I had at least looked.

His cell phone was on my plan and I could have seen whom he was calling and when and learned a lot from that, but I didn't look. I limited how much spying I was willing to do, but if I had really thought there was risk of harm or death I would have done whatever I had to do. I probably wouldn't have had to resort to snooping or being deceitful—I could have cultivated closeness and stayed in touch with him about his life and let him know I cared. *Communication* should have been our cornerstone.

* * *

I had grown up in deep poverty and felt out of place at school among the other kids who had nice clothes that fit and shoes without holes and I did not want Macky to experience that, so I always made sure he had some money, either cash or some virtual means, even while he was using—in retrospect, I probably made a mistake because I later learned all the money he got went to support his habit. I saw him losing weight and gave him money for food. To me, he deserved clothes and some money in his pocket when he went out with other people or to have gas in his car.

He loved his music and I wanted him to cultivate that pursuit, so when he told me he needed something, I got it for him or gave him my credit card. He probably pawned or sold some of the equipment, like the professional cymbals I bought or special frequency microphones for his drums.

"That's over at Mom's," he would always say if I asked about something missing.

When he developed an interest in photography, I gave him money for supplies and a special printer. I thought he would develop an artistic endeavor that diverted him from drugs.

He enrolled in college classes at junior colleges nearby and told me he needed tuition, and I was very happy to pay that. He told me he was trying to build his credit back and asked me to put the money into his checking account, so I did—but more than once, when the semester closed, the schools wouldn't release his grades because he hadn't paid his tuition. He insisted that he had paid but the school had somehow applied it to another term. He was so persuasive and guileless and I was so eager to believe him that I just accepted that "something went wrong." He promised to get things straightened out.

I wanted him to have a quality computer and whatever school supplies he needed and nice new books. When I was in college, I could afford only used books with marked-up or missing pages. I didn't want him to experience that and pictured him with the latest editions of clean, crisp textbooks. He never showed me the books or the receipts, and he told me they were at Patty's house. He said that his computer was stolen and that he needed another one. He told me that this or that class had lab fees, so I gave him cash.

I gave him money to go out with the other students. I never had money from kindergarten through college, and it was hard to see other kids have nice lunches their mothers had packed for them in elementary school and then, years later in college, see my friends go into the dining hall and get whatever they wanted using a dining card. I didn't want Macky to experience any of that, so I often taped twenty dollars to his bedroom door or on his steering wheel.

* * *

Macky started his addiction in late 2009 or early 2010, and he continued for years. Here and there, I either knew he was using or suspected it, even when he swore he was sober. He wore long sleeves or a sweatshirt every day, and when I asked why he told me he liked them and gave me a look that said, "Why are you asking? Don't you trust me?"

The entire time, I still gave him money. All he had to do was tell me how hard he was working to improve his life; I wanted so badly to believe him that I gave him what I could so he could continue to make progress. Maybe I felt guilty about how I had hurt him and belittled him and tried to make up for it by giving him what he wanted—mostly money.

* * *

I also brought my preconceived notions about heroin addiction when I contemplated Macky's drug use. Even though I loved him, I saw him as a criminal. I grew up perceiving heroin users as the worst of the worst, portrayed in books and media as dangerous law-breakers or outcasts who could never be trusted. Most prisoners in

America are locked up for drug-related offenses or problems caused by drug use, and I saw Macky as someone I would visit in jail one day.

I also remembered that time I had been robbed by a heroin addict who pushed a gun to my head. At least he let me go after he got the money I had on me.

In the ER, I was face-to-face every day with people on the streets who sought shelter from the cold or a chance to get food or drugs. They knew how to work the system and the words to say to get a bed inside, and I developed a hostile attitude toward people with any kind of addiction or substance use disorder, including alcohol.

* * *

What I did right for Macky was to keep on loving him. I tried my best to separate how I felt about *addiction*—a dangerous, harmful scourge—and how I felt about *him*, the tender young son I loved. I had trouble restraining my disdain for his drug use, and I'm sure he was confused at times because of the way I behaved. I couldn't help it sometimes and my anger roared out like at the music store that day. I forgave him for whatever he had done in the past no matter what he did. He forgave me, too. Our loving relationship as father and son provided a reason for him to recover. Macky's closeness with the rest of our family frayed, but he knew we were there—especially Homer, who stayed close to Macky through his darkest times and served as an unwavering beacon.

We still did some things as a family. Macky and I could enjoy something together, like attending a concert, playing a round of golf, or going to a ball game. Even time in the car together offered us a chance to laugh and connect. We jammed together in the basement, me on bass, Macky on drums, and sometimes Casey on guitar.

After one of those jam sessions, we talked about best guitarists. "Dad, I hate to disappoint you, but Jimi Hendrix was overrated."

After another session, when I asked about a book by David Foster Wallace, he said, "You're not ready for that."

We went to a Red Sox game at Fenway, and he spent most of the time out in the bleacher seats because he wanted to be near his favorite player, Jackie Bradley Jr., "because he's a gentleman with manners. I respect him."

* * *

I searched hard for recovery options and persuaded him to try several even though none worked. I searched the best medical literature, but I couldn't find what kind of treatment for addiction is effective. I found repetitive studies on overprescribing, alarming information about overdoses, and alternatives to opioids but nothing about *treatment*.

Some doctors responded with kindness, but each said there was nothing they could do. Answers varied among the doctors I approached.

"I can't do anything, but I hope he finds help."

"I don't know how to treat addiction."

"We're way too busy for that."

If anyone had come to me asking for help back then, I might have said, "Have you tried rehab?" because I didn't know about treatment, either.

I knew Macky's addiction wasn't the fault of any physician. They couldn't treat him because they didn't know how. At least I discovered the *need* for physician education about addiction.

I read repeated claims by detox and rehab facilities through their ubiquitous advertising and the internet, but I couldn't find any reliable science to support their assertions. I learned from high-quality medical literature that detox and rehab facilities do *not* help patients achieve recovery, with very few exceptions. Most people who go to detox or rehab will be back again and again until their insurance runs out. Untold numbers will never recover if detox or rehab is their only treatment, and they will ultimately wind up dead. That's what the most reliable medical literature confirms—repeated detox and rehab stays *increase* the likelihood of overdose death.

I took care of Macky the best I could even though much of what I did was wrong—giving him money, the latitude to make his own decisions, and the freedom to come and go as he pleased. But I also gave him a home, food, clothing, and support as I tried to build a foundation for his life. As time went on, I felt that giving Macky a place to continue using was becoming more and more dangerous unless I could find a pathway to recovery in time. I wanted to protect him but feared I might come home one day and find him dead.

I had to take care of *myself* so I could care for him. That meant medical care, psychiatric support, nutrition, exercise, and recreation. I took care of my other kids. I did my best for Anne, but I can't claim I was warm to Patty.

The things I believe I did right for Macky were to give him love, connection, forgiveness, and continued involvement with his life as I searched for effective solutions.

* * *

When Macky became addicted, I never thought about his genetic predisposition or the abuse he endured growing up while caught in the middle between warring parents. I didn't think about his easy access to cheap, powerful pills—he could buy potent, addictive opioids from friends, through school, through the internet, or on his phone.

I thought of his addiction as a personal choice, a new decision each time to get high instead of being responsible and facing life. I believed his addiction was entirely his fault, not mine. My anger made his problem worse. Fighting with Patty made his problem far more dangerous. I should have taken the time to understand why he was using, then worked with his mother and the rest of our family to learn how and where to find care. I should have told him that nothing mattered more to me than his well-being.

I wish I had said, "Macky, I'm going to help you, whatever it takes. If I have to be late for work or lose my job or lose my house or anything else along the way, I don't want to lose *you*."

And I would have said, "My bedroom door will be open tonight and every night from now on. If you tap on that door and need me, I'm going to get up and take you wherever you need to go for treatment and do whatever I can to support you. I'm going to take care of you because I love you. Just wake me up and say, 'Hey, Dad?' and I'll know why you're there. That's my promise to you."

6

Recovery

EVERYTHING MACKY AND I TRIED EITHER FAILED OR BACKFIRED, and he couldn't stop using. That's why the psychologist in Boston had told me "there's no other option" except to kick Macky out and hope for the best. If there were other options, I didn't know about them and neither did the addiction psychologist.

I thought about how treatment of diseases like cancer or heart disease improves over time through meticulous study by dedicated researchers. Patients can then trust what their doctor recommends for treatment. But I couldn't find *any* guidance about substance use disorder treatment.

Back then, addiction research was unreliable. When Macky needed help for addiction there were nearly a million doctors in the United States but only a few *hundred* who treated addiction, now known medically as substance use disorder. Most counties in the United States at that time didn't have even *one* doctor who could prescribe the right medications to treat opioid addiction.

Gradually, medications were shown to be the best way to help people recover from addiction, but the only one I ever heard about was methadone. However, no doctor in America is allowed to prescribe methadone for addiction unless it is through a handful of federally approved programs. The draconian laws restricting methadone treatment were enacted fifty years earlier during the Nixon administration and were never updated or changed even as millions of Americans developed opioid addiction and overdose deaths soared. When Macky needed help, if a doctor tried to prescribe him methadone for addiction outside of one of these centers, that doctor could be arrested and imprisoned for helping Macky. That's still true.

At the same time, I prescribe methadone every day to manage *pain*. It's one of the most common medications we use in hospice and any doctor can prescribe it right from the office without restriction as long as the purpose is to treat pain. But Nixon's laws forbid doctors from prescribing methadone—the exact same medication—to treat *addiction* unless it is given at a federal treatment center. Federal law, not medical judgment, controls how methadone can be used to treat addiction, and doctors must obey those legal restrictions or face jail.

Macky wasn't eligible for treatment with methadone because of those laws and restrictions. Even if he had been accepted into a program, we would have had to have spent four to six hours every day getting back and forth to Boston and then waited in line while being jeered at by onlookers who hated everybody standing on the "methadone mile" waiting for a dose. Maybe we should have tried that, but Macky said he wouldn't live his life that way.

I was out of options by May 2014, when I locked him out. I just hoped he would survive the night and somehow find recovery.

* * *

Macky's death would have been my fault because I had abandoned him. He was going to turn twenty-one in a few days and was probably looking forward to a little family party with his favorite supper, then a birthday cake and presents. Maybe that would have been a turning point, a time for a new start, but nothing had worked before and I didn't think a birthday party was going to change anything. If I had relented, the cycle would have continued. Maybe he would have changed his ways if he had found work or quit using if his brothers could have helped him pull himself together—they were so close growing up that maybe they could find a way. But his brothers learned they couldn't do anything about Macky's behaviors. They never stopped loving him, and both Casey and Homer did their best to persuade him to stop but Macky wouldn't listen.

Even on the day I locked Macky out, I still hoped he would decide he had had enough of life as a heroin user and quit on his own. That hope was fading and I thought he would wind up on the streets, in prison, and probably dead one day from an overdose. Second-guessing my decision wouldn't stop any of that. The addiction psychologist made it clear I had to be strong and *had* to lock him out and not let him back. There was no other choice, he said. If I didn't kick Macky out in a last-ditch effort to force him to stop, I *would* find him dead in bed. That was a chance I couldn't take because I didn't know of any other way to help him. I can still hear the slap of the deadbolt that morning.

Even if he did somehow recover and find his way back, I didn't know if he could ever forgive me for locking him out of our home and leaving him on the street penniless with nowhere to turn.

* * *

The instant I locked Macky out, I was suddenly the only one left at home. Anne and I had separated the year before because she couldn't take the way I treated her anymore. I had directed my frustrations and hostility at her as my internal turmoil escalated. Anne was the only one who stayed close to me through the grinding trauma of Macky's addiction, while at the same time she dealt with the outfall from my vicious divorce from Patty that somehow still continued.

Instead of appreciating Anne's love and sacrifices, I unleashed my frustrations at her because she was the only person still in my orbit. One day, she reached her limit and got her own place in Boston.

We didn't divorce, and we stayed in close contact and became unexpectedly warm and tender again once she had some distance from me and my troubled life. But on the day I kicked Macky out, Anne was gone and as far as I knew might never be coming back. Homer and Casey had moved away to college, and Cuff was in medical school. When Cuff came over for dinner one night, she softly said, "Dad, you need to move to something small. You know we're never coming back, right?"

Our house used to be busy and fun, but on that day in May 2014, I was alone and adrift. The rooms echoed from my footsteps. It suddenly didn't matter anymore if there was food in the refrigerator. I didn't need to watch for sales on school supplies or make sure the back door was unlocked for when the kids got home. I tried to pull myself together and think about what to make for dinner that night but then remembered there was nobody to cook for.

I made a cup of tea and sat at the kitchen table. For the first time, I could hear the soft ticking of the pale-green clock Anne had left behind.

* * *

The day Macky left, I broke off all contact with him and wouldn't read his texts, answer his calls, or open his letters. At least I knew he was still alive when I saw his attempts, and one day I decided to read one of his letters, written just eight days after he was gone. He said he had completely stopped heroin, but I wouldn't believe him anymore. I had started to learn more about heroin addiction and didn't think *anyone* could quit just like that.

Later, I learned he told me the truth in that letter. The same day I locked him out, Macky *did* stop using and started his recovery from addiction. I refused to believe that anyone could just suddenly stop injecting heroin after using it every day for years—he would have gone into intense withdrawal and relapse the same day. I had seen him try that before and saw how horrible it was. There were other times when he paced around, jittery and anxious, scratching all over, looking terrible. He told me later that happened on days when he had to wait longer than usual for heroin because he ran out of money and had to scrounge for any kind of a fix or when his dealer was late—any delay at all quickly led to withdrawal and uncontrollable cravings. I couldn't imagine there was any way he could stop just like that.

He had also told me many times before that he had quit using, and at first I believed him. I believed him the next time and the time after that—but not anymore.

But there *was* a way he could stop using in one day without going into withdrawal, with the diffuse body pains, intense trembling, vomiting, crying and moaning, and craving heroin however he could get it. It turned out that all he needed was a medication I had never heard of called Suboxone. He told me later that he had gone to Patty's house after leaving mine that day and started calling every medical treatment option he could think of to try to find a doctor who would prescribe him Suboxone. He located one in Framingham, about an hour away. The doctor agreed to see him the same day, so he made his way out there and somehow got a prescription for Suboxone.

"What's Suboxone?" I asked.

"You don't know?"

"No. I told you before that I don't every drug there is, Macky."

89

"How can you not know about Suboxone? You're a pain doctor. It's a pain medicine but works to treat addiction, too," he told me. "Jeez, Dad."

"Well, I never heard of it. None of those addiction treatment places, psychologists, or doctors ever said anything about it. Why wouldn't they tell us about a medicine that works like that?"

He shrugged his shoulders and turned up his hands.

"I don't know. You're the doctor."

"Yeah, but I don't treat addiction. I thought there was just detox, rehab, meetings—all that stuff we tried. I knew about methadone, but you didn't want that life and I didn't think you would be eligible for treatment with it anyway because the rules are so strict. The whole time there was another medicine that helps? It's hard to believe, Macky."

"Yeah, Dad. It's so weird that I have to teach you. You're right about methadone. I don't want 'liquid handcuffs' and I'm not going to that methadone clinic in Boston every day for the rest of my life. The Suboxone supposedly works even better—and I don't have to go somewhere every day for it. I just fill the prescription and use it once a day at home. It's a little film strip I dissolve in my mouth, and I'm good until the next day. I don't feel anything from it—just *normal*. I have to go to group, too, but that's no big deal."

"Well, it's still hard to believe something like that was around but nobody told us. Is it something new?"

"No. It's been around for years."

He was right. It had been out since 2002, but who knew that?

"Why didn't you tell me about it before, then?"

"I wasn't ready to stop," he said. "And I didn't think you would listen anyway."

* * *

We had first sought treatment years before, back in 2008. That's when we went to the social work drug counselor because of Macky's marijuana use and drinking. She tried to work with him, but he resisted and she couldn't help him.

His teachers and guidance counselor at school tried to help in 2009 and 2010 by being supportive and understanding and trying to get him to redirect his life. As much as they cared, they were educators, not therapists. They couldn't get him to stop using. Macky appreciated their kindness and even wrote a personal letter to one expressing his gratitude for her concern. He told her not to worry and that he was going to be fine.

Once I knew he was addicted in late 2010 and realized he couldn't quit on his own, I looked for help. I searched the internet like everybody else, but I couldn't afford those faraway rehab centers and doubted they worked anyway. The one in Massachusetts we tried when he was seventeen was a nightmare and I never wanted to go near one again. The local detox had turned us away at the door and soured my opinion on what they do. I wasn't going to take him to anymore bogus rehabs or detox facilities where the concern is making money, not helping patients.

Neither of us found any benefit from the meetings we attended, especially at big academic centers. We spent hours driving to them, searching for parking, then listening to speakers who seemed to know less about addiction than we did. I found out much later that just a few buildings away from where we were sitting in a small auditorium for a lecture one evening, there was a clinic Macky could have walked into any day of the week and asked for help with stopping his addiction. He would have seen a medical doctor experienced in addiction care, and he could have been started on effective treatment with medications then and there.

Between 2010 and 2014, we tried everything we could think of and afford. I resorted to force, using threats and emotional brutality, resorting to cruelty. I eventually realized that my rough treatment *never* helped him—I only hurt his progress and pushed him into more secrecy and increased use, but maybe at some level at least he knew I cared.

There were times I was kind and accepting, and *that's* when he listened to me and opened up. He told me how he wanted to stop but couldn't, how he regretted what he had done but didn't know what to do. He apologized for hurting me and the rest of the family and cried when he relived things he had done but could never undo. Those were our closest moments, and he was willing to accept help—we just didn't know how to *find* it.

* * *

I still struggled with the question of why medical schools and postgraduate residency training programs refused to incorporate teaching about the devastating new threat of death by overdose. I just couldn't fathom why this subject was absent from the curriculum at every medical school in the United States. If it was taught anywhere, I never heard about it. There was not one single question on my licensing exams or board certification tests about addiction treatment.

Most Americans don't know that every doctor at every medical school in America is *required* to learn the basics of surgery, obstetrics and gynecology, pediatrics, psychiatry, and a host of other areas to graduate, even if they will later become radiologists or eye doctors. Every doctor, no matter what they specialize in later, must meet certain training requirements in place at every American medical school—but those educational requirements didn't provide even basic understanding of what was happening, except to teach that some doctors had been duped into overprescribing.

After medical school, doctors then have to spend three to six more years in residency training (often working more than a hundred hours a week) to become specialists in their field, but in all those years, there was *still* no teaching about treating addiction. Addiction medicine wasn't recognized as a formal specialty by the American Board of Medical Specialties until 2016, years after Macky and I searched in vain for help.

To renew their medical license every two or three years, doctors have to spend forty, fifty, or more hours every year keeping up with advances and changes in medicine through what's called continuing medical education (CME). When opioid overprescribing swelled and overdose deaths accelerated, states started to require that a few of those CME hours be spent learning "safe opioid prescribing" but did not require anyone to know anything about "treating addiction." That's why it was so difficult for Macky to find help.

To me, the content of those safe opioid-prescribing courses translated to *no* opioid prescribing. That left millions of patients with pain to suffer when effective treatment was available. There were no training modules I encountered that taught that opioids are effective when prescribed by judicious, knowledgeable clinicians for legitimate medical purposes with mitigated risk if the prescriber knows how to use them with caution and maintains a watchful eye.

Macky learned more about Suboxone from the street than I learned in all my years of training to become a physician and then a specialist in pain management.

* * *

When he started taking Suboxone, I didn't know how it worked or why. I always researched professional medical resources when someone in my family needed treatment, so I tried to learn about Suboxone. My resources linked to information about the active ingredient, called buprenorphine, and from there everything I found talked about its use in pain management. I had never used it for pain management in my hospice and palliative care practice because we have far better medicines to manage pain. I couldn't find clear answers about how Suboxone works to treat opioid addiction, but even though I didn't know how or why it worked, what I cared about most was that it helped Macky. He had stopped using heroin and started to put his life back together.

He called me again, but I still wasn't ready to answer, even though it had been months since we talked. I let his call roll over to voice mail and decided to listen instead of delete it. His call came in on December 22, 2014.

"Hey, Dad, how's it going'? Um, I just wanted to touch base with you, and also I just wanted to let you know—I've got a job! Um, so yeah, I just wanted to talk to you, so if you could call me back, that'd be great. Alright? Thanks. Love you."

Homer, Macky's older brother and most steadfast friend, had kept Macky close, spent time with him, and did his best to keep him focused on recovery. Homer wanted Macky to reconnect with the rest of our family.. Homes called me the very next day after I got Macky's voice mail. He wanted to talk about plans we had made to have dinner at my house.

"Is it cool if Macky comes over, too? He's doing really well, Dad."

"Sure, I'd love to see him. It's been a while."

"Great! See you tomorrow, then!" he said.

When they came over, Macky was warm and gentle, the way he was before drugs. I could hardly believe what I saw. His eyes were bright, his clothes were clean, and his behavior was polite. He talked about books he was reading with clear, thoughtful speech.

"How about you, Dad? How's everything?" he asked.

We talked for hours and he told me about his plans for the future, getting his GED, and going back to school but this time with a purpose. He loved his job because he was trusted and appreciated—and earning his own money. His joy at work reminded me of how happy I felt at my first job, washing dishes at a chicken diner. I had friends there, food, and a paycheck, and I loved it, so I understood his happiness.

He soon started coming over more, usually with one of his brothers for dinner or to watch a game together. Pretty soon, I wanted to have him back in my life.

"Macky, you can stay the night if you want," I said one day.

"Thanks, Dad. That would be nice."

"I know how hard you're trying, and you're doing really well. That's what I was hoping for. I'm serious, you can come over whenever you want."

"You sure?"

"Yes, Macky. Let's just keep things cool and you let me know if something comes up. If anything happens, we'll get through it together. Okay?"

He brought his drums back over and soon he was living with me again. He had been using an old car Patty shared with him for his job delivering pizzas, and he was proud to be valued by the owners of the little pizzeria. When he moved in with me, he used a beat-up old truck I had for work after we riveted on pieces of sheet metal to cover the rust holes. He never missed a day of work, going out in the freezing cold or pouring rain without complaining except once when water got into his shoes and froze. He brought books in for the Greek owners to share with their children to learn more

English. Macky brought in his own books once he finished them and set up a small library in their store.

He took his music more seriously and found other committed musicians, and at times he let me play with them even though I didn't know his complex rhythms. I never expected to hear us making music together again. Macky started rebuilding his life in ways I thought I would never see again.

* * *

He needed his Suboxone each morning, and at first he was private about it. I knew it was some kind of synthetic opioid even though it was only a "partial" one, different from street drugs and the potent opioids I prescribed for my patients. He told me it didn't cause any kind of high or euphoria; it just shut off his need for heroin or any other opioid. I knew that by itself it would not cause an overdose, but I still thought it might be affecting him in some negative way.

Even though Macky was functional and happy again, I had the same notion that a lot of people in rehab programs or AA believed. I thought he was "trading one addiction for another" and I wanted him to stop. The current definition of addiction, which I didn't know at the time, includes the words "increasing use despite negative consequences." Macky was *decreasing* how much Suboxone he used and achieving *positive* results. He was not addicted to Suboxone and neither were other patients taking it as prescribed. Diabetics are not "addicted" to insulin or similar medications they use, and they are obviously not addicted to it. They are *dependent* on insulin to stay healthy and that's what Suboxone is like. I just didn't realize that at the time or have any other medical understanding of addiction, either.

"Macky, how much of that stuff are you taking?"

"I started at thirty-two milligrams. That's the highest dose. I'm down to sixteen now."

"When are you going to stop?"

"I don't know. That's up to the doctor."

"Can't you just stop using it on your own? Tell him you don't want to be on drugs?"

"No. If I stop suddenly I'll go into withdrawal just like you saw happen before," he said.

"So that means you're *addicted* to it—how is that different than heroin?"

"I'm not addicted to it and I wish you wouldn't say that, Dad. It's a medicine that helps me *not* be addicted."

Even though I loved seeing Macky flourish, I didn't like how he still needed a drug to function. Any drug. He was no longer the wayward, rebellious teenager I knew before or the raging "drug addict" I saw him become. He had quietly developed into a sensitive, caring young man. All those horrible behaviors when he was using heroin had stopped, and he restructured his whole life in a new direction—but I hadn't changed *my* attitude about drug use and still believed Macky was making a choice and could stop that stuff if he really wanted to.

I prescribed powerful opioids to my patients in severe pain caused by advanced cancer or some other awful disease because they needed them. They didn't "choose" to get sick, and it wasn't their fault they needed these drugs every day. But Macky *did* make a choice to use drugs when he first started, and I couldn't let go of that—I wouldn't accept his addiction as substance use disorder, illness, or disease no matter what the science showed. That was a grave mistake.

* * *

He had to see the doctor every week and pay up front or he wouldn't be seen or get his prescription. There were times he could borrow a car from Patty or me, but he usually took the train out there, one that allowed him to take his bike onboard so he could pedal to the doctor's office. The truck was unsafe to take on the highway. The New England weather didn't matter—he had to get out there, and if he got soaked riding his bike in the rain he just dealt with it.

I gave him cash or wrote checks to the doctor, who wouldn't accept insurance. The doctor wasn't part of a group or hospital and didn't send out bills. He demanded the money up front. The visits weren't that expensive, about a hundred dollars a visit, and it was worth it to me to have Macky back. I wondered about this doctor's priorities. It was hard to imagine he would turn a desperate patient away at the door and risk having them return to the street and do whatever they had to for cash. Macky didn't want to talk about professionalism or risk. He just told me he *had* to be there every week with payment in hand.

I drove him out there and back a few times, but in traffic or bad weather it could take more than two hours. By far, the shortest part of the trip was the visit with the doctor.

"You can leave the car running, Dad. I'll be out in five minutes."

"But what about your exam and checking on how you're doing?"

"Dad, are you kidding? The only thing he checks is if I have the money."

My concerns about Suboxone worsened as I saw how Macky *had* to have his daily dose. With a new prescription every week he learned which pharmacies stocked the medication in the dose he needed, but even that varied. None of our local pharmacies had it, not even the ones owned by big chains. He tried calling the pharmacies first to find out if they had it in stock but often got lost in a series of phone prompts.

I overheard some of those calls. When he finally reached a person and asked about Suboxone in specific doses and how much they had, whoever answered the phone was cold to him. They knew that Suboxone treated heroin addiction, and they had the same disdain for drug addiction that the general public does.

"We don't give out that information," one said.

"I understand," Macky said. "I just want to be sure you have it because it's a long drive and my family has to bring me."

"We don't discuss our controlled substances."

"I know, miss. I don't want to be rude or anything. It would just really help me to know before we drive there."

"Please hold," the person would say, but then nobody picked up.

Someone in our family would then have to drive him to Worcester and wait with him in line at different pharmacies. He couldn't use the truck to get to the pharmacies because it was on its last legs and we had to keep it going for his job. All of us took turns getting him to Worcester, but it was mostly me. Macky would direct me to the big pharmacies. He really knew the back roads and alleys in Worcester, especially Main South in Worcester, a scary area at the time.

"Make a left here. Cut across that dirt strip by the warehouse. And stop worrying, Dad. I can feel it."

"How do you know these places?" I asked.

He didn't answer and kept giving directions.

One day, there was a big playoff game we had been waiting for. Our team, the New England Patriots, were in a championship game.

"I need my medicine, Dad."

"You're just now realizing that? When the game's about to start?"

"Sorry. It won't take long."

"It won't take long to drive to Worcester and wait in line on a Sunday? And *this* Sunday, when the game is about to start?"

"I told you I was sorry. What am I supposed to do?"

I drove him there, fuming the whole time as we went to three different pharmacies. I turned mean.

"This is for your fucking *drugs*. The drugs you said you're not addicted to but you can't stop. That's what addiction *is*, Macky! Now we miss the Patriots game to go stand in line and pay for the stuff. This is *not* how I want to live!"

I felt like I was going to explode. There was nothing Macky could say or do to calm me down. He meekly presented his prescription, hoping they would have the medicine. One finally did, and he showed them his driver's license. He had to turn around and look at me when they told him how much it cost, then ask me for money to pay for it.

* * *

Patty didn't understand Suboxone, either. She was a registered nurse, and I met her in the ER when I was in training. She still worked as a nurse but didn't know about addiction, either, because just like physicians, that was never part of nurse education. Macky called me in a panic one day while he was staying with her while I was away for the weekend.

"I need your help, Dad. It's really important."

"What's going on?"

"I'm at Mom's. She took my Suboxone bottle when I was asleep and hid it somewhere, and now she can't remember where she put it. I'm already getting sick."

"Why would she do that? She knows you need it, right?"

"No, Dad. She doesn't understand, but that doesn't matter right now. I'm getting bad fast. Can you call me in a script? Please?"

"I can't prescribe controlled substances for my own family, Macky, and *that* one would really set them off. I could lose my license."

I could hear Patty in the background say, "You need to get off that drug. *That's* why you're sick!"

There was nothing I could do. Macky left Patty's, and I knew that one way or the other he had to find Suboxone from someone in a hurry. Or find heroin.

* * *

I pressed him to stop the Suboxone and avoid all this trouble but he insisted that it wasn't that simple. I tracked down more information in the medical literature and learned more about how it works. The opioid ingredient in Suboxone—buprenorphine—goes straight to the brain receptors, where heroin and other opioids attach and it completely blocks those receptors. That's why patients who suffer from heroin addiction can stop heroin in the space of one day, just like Macky told me. The Suboxone is started and heroin withdrawal and cravings stop—as long as the patient *continues* the Suboxone every day. I also found out that Suboxone is *not* a magic bullet in overcoming heroin addiction. It works for most people with addiction, but many patients will relapse or just stop taking it. But years of medical literature strongly support that Suboxone and methadone are the most effective treatments we have for heroin addiction today.

Nevertheless, I kept haranguing Macky about it. I didn't think he should need to be taking it the rest of his life, so I thought he should just get to work on stopping it as soon as possible. I wanted him to be drug free.

"How much are you on now?" I asked.

"Still sixteen. It takes a long time to taper it down."

"So what does that mean? How long are you going to be using it?"

"I don't know," he answered.

"Macky, I told you I don't want you to be on drugs—not *any* kind of drug. You're doing so well it's time to stop."

"No. That's not how it works. It's not hurting me. And why is it such a big deal to you?"

"How do you *know* it isn't hurting you or doing something bad to you that we don't know about yet?"

"It *is* doing something—it's keeping me off heroin," he said. "Isn't that enough?"

We went back and forth for months as I tried to compel him to stop his medication. It wasn't just all those trips to the doctor and the pharmacies, and it wasn't the cost. I was worried about seeing him dependent on a medication every day, especially one I didn't understand.

* * *

Something unexpected happened to get him to stop. I was studying my medical resources about certain opioids I had to combine for one of my patients, and I read about the potential side effects. For doctors, that literature is easy to interpret because every possible side effect is listed and doctors know which ones are common enough to matter. It's similar to the long list of things that pharmaceutical companies say at the end of their new-product commercials, stating how some new drug "may cause blah, blah, blah . . . or death," blurted out as fast as possible in a garbled whisper.

Then I saw in my literature source that one of the potential side effects of opioids is suppression of the hormones involved in sexual desire and performance.

We were sitting in my kitchen and I decided to show Macky that page on my computer. He read it, then snapped the laptop shut.

"That's it. I'm getting off Suboxone."

"Whoa, wait a minute. Not *that* fast. You said it had to be reduced a little at a time."

"Yeah, well, that time is starting right now. The next time I see the doctor I'm telling him I'm going to stop it."

"That's good, but you're going to be careful, right?"

"I'm going to stop it, Dad. You just showed me all I needed to know."

Within another month or so, I found a handwritten note from Macky taped to my bedroom door when I got up for work.

"Today's my last visit with the Suboxone doctor. I just need some money for the train and the hundred bucks to pay him. I have to get my last prescription and then I'm all done! Thanks, Dad! Love you!" he wrote.

It was hard for him to wean off that last two-milligram dose during his last week of use and he suffered with it. But he was resolute and wouldn't surrender to the waxing and waning withdrawal symptoms that simmered the whole time. He didn't give in and finally was off Suboxone.

I was happy to see him drug free for the first time in so many years even though the last one, Suboxone, was neither a "drug of abuse" nor a "recreational drug." It was a medication approved by the U.S. Food and Drug Administration that had been proven to treat opioid addiction, and it helped him stop heroin—the demon that haunted him daily, even in his dreams, as he once wrote.

What I did not understand at the time was that Suboxone prevented *withdrawal* symptoms but did not stop his *addiction*. His brain function had changed with years of opioid use and would take years to return to normal. Macky needed time for those brain changes to resolve, and the Suboxone was giving him that time—until I made him stop. His extreme risk of returning to opioid use was still there. But now the critical opioid receptors that had been blocked by Suboxone were wide open again. Any trigger could put him right back where he started—or worse.

7

Hope

WHEN MACKY STARTED LIFE IN RECOVERY FROM ADDICTION, HE gradually constructed the pillars that would sustain his progress. He discovered the critical importance of structure, work, relationships, support, purpose, and goals. Aspects that were previously invisible surfaced, including the warmth of living at home with me again; helping out with cooking and cleaning; enjoying hobbies like reading, writing, and playing sports; and having a car to get to school and work. He had lost track of the beautiful emotions of life during his years of descent into addiction, but one by one, the feelings of joy, hope, and self-confidence returned. With even the smallest achievements, such as making us supper or getting his homework done on time, I started to see him smile again. He walked tall, wore clean clothes, and combed his hair. When he started to laugh again over little inside jokes, I realized how long it had been since I heard his gentle voice softly chuckling.

He also faced many impediments to his recovery. He had easy access to dangerous drugs and knew how to get them fast, so every time he encountered adversity he had to resist turning to heroin with a single call or text and be right back into his blissful nightmare. Relapse seemed inevitable as he tried to find his way in life, but he still fought hard against ever using opioids again. He dealt with disdain from people who would neither forgive him nor forget what he had done. He was unprepared for the everyday challenges of life because he spent so much of his adulthood using a needle as his only defense and suddenly had to learn how to cope and survive. When he was shunned by people he had thought cared about him or faced heartache as he searched for love, I sometimes found him crying alone in his room. I couldn't help him except to tell him how much I loved him and promise him I would always be there for him. I don't know how much that helped him, but that was the truth and I hoped he knew that.

I realized later that I continued to make mistakes that threatened to derail his momentum. I didn't watch him closely and tell him that I *had* to do that to help keep him safe. I never accepted my responsibility to learn about addiction or what worked to achieve and sustain recovery so I could work with him along the way. I didn't look into what causes relapse or learn what to do if that happened. I thought his addiction was over, so I didn't even have Narcan around if he used again and overdosed.

* * *

Only a week after Macky's recovery started when I kicked him out on May 19, 2014, he decided to send me an email, dated May 26. He had just turned twenty-one three days before. I wanted to believe him, but after all we had been through, I couldn't. He tried hard to convince me but probably knew he couldn't.

Dear Father,
I remember how you expressed that I should not attempt to contact you and of course that is deserved by me. I sincerely hope that you take the time to read this note with whatever sympathy and patience you might have left for me. I have not touched that which has for so long crippled my mind, blinded, numbed, and deafened me, since the day after I last saw you. Early sobriety is naturally proving to be an exceedingly difficult ordeal for myself and those around me. There is a line from Othello

that has been particularly helpful, "How poor are they that have not patience! What wound did ever heal but by degrees?"

I do not aim to earn your respect, trust, and belief in me with mere words. The objective of this letter is simply to relate to you my dire need of a solid anchor, to which I shall secure and protect myself from the sirens that haunt me daily and stalk me even in my dreams. I have been to the underworld and I have made it back across the river Styx, but I am not yet home.

With love and absolute sincerity,
Your son,
Max

He was correct that "mere words" would not be enough to assure me that he was already in recovery from addiction, but I was glad to hear from him.

I wrote him back the same day.

Dear Macky:
I'm glad you wrote to me with such care and warmth—it was very nice to hear from you. As I hope you know, my first concern is definitely for your health and well-being. My affection for you remains as strong as the day you were born, and that will never change.

Please forgive yourself for whatever you've done in the past and let go of the painful feelings you have for whatever you've done. None of those things can be changed, so I hope you'll just look towards the future, one day at a time—but you still have to face up to these things. I need to know you are doing everything in your power to achieve your goals as demonstrated by your actions.

You have my care and concern, and that will never end. I think about you constantly and long for your return to health.

With hope and everlasting affection,
Dad

* * *

While he was still taking Suboxone in 2014, Macky had found a job, the one he told me about in his voicemail, delivering pizzas for a small pizzeria in Clinton, fifteen minutes from Sterling. The owners trusted him with money and knew he would always show up for work on time, then be polite to the customers when he went to their homes. He had a regular schedule, a small but reliable paycheck, and a deep appreciation for the immigrant owners who had given him a chance to prove himself. He told me again how he brought in children's books to help the owners' kids improve their English and reading confidence. He loved repeating that he also read his own books in between deliveries, long and difficult books that he liked ever since he discovered the beauty of classic literature and then left his books at the pizzeria and created a small library so that customers could take a glance at quality writing while waiting for their food. Landing that job thrilled Macky.

I understood his joy because my first job was washing dishes at a fried chicken restaurant in Glendale, California, when I was thirteen—I got free food every day and learned some basic cooking from Sammy the chef. I loved the charm of the smiling waitresses, the sound of their lilting voices, and the alluring scent of their perfume. I might have worked there for free, but I was very happy to get a paycheck every week. The source of Macky's satisfaction—trust and responsibility—was different, but he was happy for the first time in a long time.

He decided to complete his GED in 2014. He had dropped out of high school when he was sixteen and knew he couldn't get far without an education. He studied for the exam and proudly showed me his certificate when he got it. That opened the door for him to enroll at Quinsigamond Junior College and take more challenging classes. His English professor would later turn out to be mine, too, when I decided to take classes there for pleasure.

I asked Macky if I could see some of his work. He showed me complex essays about esoteric history and the meaning behind ancient literature. His papers were carefully organized and written with clarity and depth. I discovered a list of some of his favorite authors, including Kafka, Hemingway, Nabokov, Homer, Dostoevsky, and others, along with writers of dark crime fiction. Macky no longer used school as a way to trick me into giving him money. He attended school to learn and improve his life.

He accompanied me one day on a trip to the Massachusetts State House, where I had been invited to a daytime event. Macky wore a suit and tie and beamed on the Senate floor beneath the golden dome on Beacon Hill in Boston. A legislator saw his delight and took him on a tour, showing him paintings of heroes from the Revolutionary War and statues of leaders like George Washington. A few days later, he told me about a new plan.

"Dad, I want to run for office. I want to be in the Student Senate at school."

I went with him once when he campaigned on campus, wearing a shirt and tie, shaking hands and asking for votes. He won, and in his acceptance speech he quoted Theodore Roosevelt's oratory from 1910, "The Man in the Arena."

"The credit belongs to the man who is actually in the arena, whose face is marred by dust and sweat and blood; who strives valiantly; who errs, who comes up short again and again, because there is no effort without error and shortcoming."

Macky had certainly been marred and had erred and come up short again and again. But he learned from his mistakes and was back on track with determination and purpose.

* * *

He continued to build structure and flourish. He reconnected with Ryan, his bass player who had remained understanding through Macky's worst years. Together, they found other committed musicians and practiced at scheduled times. They found studio space and later started recording, then cut some tracks during jam sessions.

Macky had resisted drum lessons because the instructors wanted him to learn drum rudiments, the basic patterns and structure underlying all rhythms. He had always wanted to do things his own way and managed to become proficient, but sometime in 2014 or 2015, he focused on rudiments until he finally had the patterns down. I wondered if learning the basic patterns and structure essential to excellence on the drums carried over to the rest of his life.

* * *

Macky followed his big brother Homer everywhere, starting when Macky crawled around the house as a baby. Homer was exactly two years older and loved having Macky by his side. They fought so fiercely as little boys that there were times I couldn't bear to watch, but two minutes later they would be outside playing and laughing. Homer taught Macky, even as a toddler, how to use our computer to play simple games with the arrow keys. He kept on teaching Macky throughout his childhood, helping him with his homework and teaching him how to hit a baseball and how to behave around girls once they reached that age.

When Macky veered into his earliest drug use in 2005 or so, Homer saw trouble and worried. But Macky made his own decisions by then and had started new friendships, so as much as Homer didn't like what he saw his little brother doing, he put up with it because he couldn't stop it. They started to drift apart some but never disconnected. They moved in parallel worlds with separate activities but remained close most of the time. Distance increased when Homer had a steady girlfriend by 2006, and he saw more and more of her, which meant less and less time with Macky.

Both knew they had to keep certain things secret from me because I would have flamed out had I known, like what they did on vacation together or what went on in the house when I was at work. I didn't need to know the details about first kisses or sipping alcohol to know those were things teenagers did. They had asked me over and over again about what *I* did as a teen during the 1960s, but my answer was always, "Things were different back then." As a teenager I had lived on the farthest edge I could reach without hurting anybody or getting arrested. My children didn't need to know what that meant.

Little by little, the boys were doing more of their own things with each passing year. By 2009, Homer left for college. He and Macky still saw each other at times, but during Homer's college years, until 2012, Macky had more or less become a loner—from the family anyway.

Homer saw Macky's severe downward spiral but couldn't stop him. He also saw how rough I was with Macky and how other people treated Macky since he had become a *heroin addict*, shunned by everyone as he skirted the law, lying and stealing his way through life. Homer was probably the one person who never changed his feelings toward Macky and saw him as the little brother he loved, not a derelict or outcast. Macky knew that, and when he stopped using in 2014 he looked to Homer, who had never turned on him.

Macky learned that his best friend always was—and always would be—Homer. I saw Homer get upset with Macky at times and chastise him when he slipped up, but I always saw him behave with firmness instead of cruelty. Macky responded to that guidance, and I tried to emulate that style. I had never learned strength and stability as a parent, and I had a palette of black and white—kindness and fury with not much in between.

Homer's support of Macky's recovery never wavered. Homer opened the door to Macky coming back into my life, which I had resisted and thought I might never do. I saw the same thing in Casey, my oldest son, who learned to accept that Macky's life in addiction was in the past and that the right thing to do was help him continue to rebuild.

Anne and I had never broken up even though she still had her own place outside Boston where she stayed sometimes. I stayed there off and on, too, because I missed her. She never anticipated what she was in for when she married me in 2007. Macky's addiction was even worse than my continued divorce wrangling, which still hadn't stopped even all those years later. She understood Macky's problems better than I did, and as he worked to improve his life she gave him emotional support and reliability that never veered into frustration or anger toward him. He knew what she expected from him—truth, accountability, and promises kept.

I did my best to support his recovery, too, *after* I had turned my back on him for months at risk of overdose or whatever might happen to a young person alone on the streets. When Macky moved back in with me, I saw the enormous value of support. He suddenly had constancy in his life, with reliability and acceptance from Anne, Casey, and others. Homer gave his heart to Macky with strength and unconditional love. Homer held nothing in reserve, and I think his love was the single strongest factor in sustaining Macky's recovery.

* * *

Macky attended AA meetings sometime in 2014 as part of his recovery and also participated in group therapy sessions that same year, but he never involved me and rarely talked about what went on at AA or his therapy. I know he knew about the "twelve steps" and went along with the program, but he didn't agree that he was powerless or that he had to turn his life over to a higher power to recover. Both Macky and I accepted that millions of people who sought help with AA since its founding in 1935 said that the support and fellowship in those meetings were key to their finding sobriety. It didn't matter to either one of us if we agreed with every step because those meetings made the difference between life and death for so many people over the years.

Maybe Macky took some guidance for what he should do from listening to those twelve steps because so many of the things he did while achieving recovery reflect that list.

He took responsibility for his decisions to drink and use drugs. He blamed absolutely nobody but himself. He never claimed that he was "genetically predisposed" or had been traumatized by childhood abuse. He didn't blame Patty or me for anything and never criticized whoever it was who first gave him heroin.

There was nothing that would help him stop until he made the decision *himself* to stop. If he had been locked up or threatened with prison, he would have used again when he got out. If someone gave him a medication to stop the effect of drugs before he was ready to quit, he would have waited for it to wear off and used again. He knew that he alone could take the first step to recovery.

Macky went to those he had hurt and apologized for his actions. He never said, "I was on drugs and couldn't stop myself." He admitted that his behaviors were harmful and destructive and hoped he could help heal those he had hurt. There were times he hoped for forgiveness, but he didn't think he deserved it.

He reached out to others at the meetings and shared what he had learned so that he could help them. He talked with people outside of the meetings if they were open to listening and tried to help them understand the dangers of drugs. It was awkward and uncomfortable to "preach," so instead he shared his own story so that others could reach their own conclusions.

He didn't make much money delivering pizza, but he bought back what he could from the pawnshops and returned them. My things were long gone, but there were a few things he could find and he did his best to get them back to their rightful owners. He had already given me what money he had to pay for my missing musical equipment—I didn't want the few dollars he worked so hard to earn, but I took it. I had to, for him.

He forgave everything I had done to hurt him: the cruelty, judgment, and erratic behaviors that left him confused or wounded. He didn't enumerate, "You did this, you did that," and he said if I had done anything to hurt him, he deserved it. I don't know what he said to Patty, but I know he appreciated all she had done for him and why she had treated him roughly when she couldn't take it anymore. I'm certain he forgave her.

He reflected back on what led to his addiction and wrote about it, but when I read it there were only words about what he had done and nothing about what was done to him. He tried to understand how it all happened, perhaps as a way to one day lead to a better understanding of addictive personalities and behaviors. Maybe he thought his insights would one day lead to prevention.

Whether or not he believed in a higher power of some sort, he respected the rights of others to their own beliefs. I know Macky believed in his own obligation to behave with dignity and accept consequences when he lost his way.

* * *

Certain elements helped him keep his focus and move forward, things I wouldn't have expected. His grades in school mattered to him even though he wasn't sure what he was going to do with his life at that time and if grades would even matter. I took all three boys on vacation to see my family in California in July 2016, and we got to use a friend's condo near the beach. Macky brought his books and computer with him because he had summer assignments he wanted to finish, but he dropped the computer and broke the screen. He asked Homer to wire the laptop to the TV in our condo. When I took the older boys out, Macky stayed behind and worked on his homework.

On the same trip, I took all three boys to watch our baseball team, the Boston Red Sox, play the California Angels in Anaheim. The afternoon game was exciting, but when I looked over at Macky he wasn't watching. He had a notebook open, doing a math assignment. He couldn't figure out a certain formula, so Casey, a physics major, took the pencil and showed him how to work through it.

It wasn't just grades and schoolwork that mattered to him. He searched for anything productive he could accomplish.

We worked on his car together and tried to fix the truck. He mowed our lawn in the summer, raked the leaves in the fall, and shoveled snow in the winter. He used an ax from the garage to split a pile of logs into cordwood for the fireplace. At one point, he went to our local gym and worked with a trainer so hard that he almost passed out. He found a book I had on nutrition for athletes, read it, and tried to follow the diet. Cooking became important to him, and he loved making meals for us. Any recipe that called for sun-dried tomatoes was exotic to him, so I made sure to have some around and give him that pleasure. He wanted to have a role and a purpose.

* * *

As he did his best to recover, he was still missing one thing to feel complete: romance.

Macky had met Emma in late 2015, when Homer took him to meet some girls he knew. Macky and Emma bonded almost immediately over literature, science, and culture. Neither of them knew that Emma had grown up for years in the same neighborhood as Macky in Sterling, only a few houses down the street. That was a family neighborhood with lots of kids, and they had never met each other or even heard about one another. Both were smitten, and within weeks they were a couple. Macky never talked about Emma's beautiful looks, tall with red hair.

"She's the most brilliant woman I ever met," he told me.

She was Macky's first love, and they were inseparable. Early on, he told her the truth about his former addiction and all the mistakes he had made in those years. She was happy he trusted her enough to reveal everything that happened and happier still that he was in recovery.

Emma came over often and was a joy to be around. She liked rock climbing like I did, but Macky didn't. The three of us went to the climbing gym together, and Emma and I belayed each other while Macky watched in between reading chapters of a thick book he was reading—like always.

Macky developed even stronger determination to stay sober and work toward meaningful goals. Emma attended college up at UMass Lowell, about an hour or two away. Macky had just graduated from Quinsigamond Junior College and decided to continue school at Lowell so he could be near her. It was too far to drive back and forth every day, so we rented a room in a beat-down house with no air conditioning and worn-out cast-off furniture. At least we could afford it, and he wouldn't have to drive.

After the summer of 2016, Emma's next semester was going to be abroad in Costa Rica. She didn't really want to go anymore because of Macky, but it had been set up and paid for long before, so she left in July 2016 for Central America. She had little time to spare while studying and almost no cell service. She had only a weak Wi-Fi signal, available at unpredictable times, so both suffered from being apart and out of touch.

Macky took it on himself to get a passport picture at the post office and then successfully obtain a passport. He found a dirt-cheap flight to Central America, flying at night with multiple stops, but it was worth it to him. He flew down there for a week with Emma.

He also saved up to buy her roses to be delivered to her down there and wrote her a poem. His gentle words became garbled in translation as he tried to communicate with the florist, who didn't speak English, but Emma eventually got the flowers and the love note.

She knew more about Macky's history than I did, but that was between them, and I never asked. I respected that she knew everything but wouldn't leave him based on his past. Her support was different than Homer's because it was based on romantic love. But like Homer, she supported Macky in maintaining his recovery forever. She was there for him in every way.

Macky showed joyful emotions that had been absent for so long that I didn't remember what his laughter sounded like. I recognized the smile I knew from when he was a little boy. He was twenty-three years old then, and I had never seen him so happy.

She came home on December 15, 2016. That's when she and Macky started to talk about wedding rings.

* * *

Throughout Macky's four years of heroin addiction, I learned a lot about family perspectives about addiction but not the *medical* understanding of it. I didn't try hard enough to learn how it happens or what to do. When he recovered, he did it on his own by searching for the medication he knew could help along with group therapy. I hadn't helped him at all.

Once he stopped using heroin by using Suboxone, I pressured him to stop using it because I didn't understand its importance in maintaining recovery and preventing death.

I brought him back into my life and did what I thought was best by offering him forgiveness, support, love, and a second chance. Those actions were important, but he needed more to avert a tragedy.

He needed more medical treatment. He had been seeing the Suboxone doctor in Framingham, who helped Macky by at least giving him the prescription he needed, but if there were any *care* involved, I couldn't detect it. We never discussed what Macky's long-term care plan should be or what I should do at home. Macky was an adult at that time, but I wish I had been given the opportunity to help with his recovery. To be fair to Macky and that doctor, I didn't request to be involved, either.

Macky had underlying emotional troubles that led him to drug use in the first place. His child psychologist had told me that Macky was at severe risk of emotional damage after growing up with years of fierce parental conflict and that the damage was probably permanent, but Macky didn't want to see anyone. There were family therapists in Boston and Worcester, but appointments were almost impossible to find. As a doctor, I knew what to say to speed up getting an appointment, but I really didn't want to go anyway.

Macky told me in a letter that through AA he had found a sponsor, someone he could call anytime if he needed help staying away from drugs or alcohol, but after he was home with me he never again mentioned going to AA or contacting his sponsor. There were similar support groups for families who had a loved one with addiction, but I didn't want anything to do with those. I went to one of those support groups once but thought that however much they helped one another, they weren't going to be able to help me so I never went again.

I had heard of "recovery coaches," people who had recovered from addiction and went on to support others in recovery, but I met only one and didn't think Macky would relate to him. I found out much later that many people in recovery from addiction find their recovery coach to be the most important person on the team.

By 2014 and 2015, more medical literature about addiction was published. I tried to learn more about the causes and treatment of addiction and what doctors need to know, but the medical literature hammered away about *overprescribing*, and that was old news. I didn't find anything useful about addiction in the medical resources I searched at that time and stopped looking.

I didn't plan what to do if something went wrong. I had promised Macky that I would help him if he relapsed, but I wasn't any more prepared than I was before. I knew what *didn't* work—detox and rehab—and had learned that Suboxone and methadone were the most effective treatments for opioid addiction, but I didn't know where I could take him in the middle of the night or even in the middle of the day. The default response of every doctor's office when there is an unexpected problem is always "go to the ER." After working there for twenty years, I knew that's exactly what patients did—go to the ER. But doctors there didn't know what to do about addiction. Their default response for addiction—and mine—was to tell the patient "go to rehab."

I gave Macky too much money. I wanted him to have some on him in case he had a flat tire, ran out of gas, or got hungry. The problem was that a dose of heroin back then cost five dollars, less than a pack of cigarettes or a six-pack of beer. I had been giving him ten or twenty dollars on days when he left for school. I should have used a credit or debit card and seen where and when it was used. Every experienced heroin user can manipulate a credit card, but nothing's easier than cash. I asked Macky once while he was in recovery if there was anything I could do to help him avoid relapse.

"Yes, Dad," he said. "Don't give me any money."

* * *

I wouldn't talk to Patty. She told me in phone calls and letters that it was time to settle our differences and put the children first, but I was so bitter that I wouldn't speak to her anymore. Macky's familiar pattern of saying, "I'm going to Mom's" remained unquestioned, like the letters of transit in the movie *Casablanca*.

Communication didn't seem necessary anyway because I was starry-eyed about Macky's recovery. There were whispers that he might still be using, but I didn't believe what I heard. He had admitted to one-time use after I found a needle in his robe, and to me his admission and apology meant he was honest and I could trust him.

That was the time when buying drugs online blossomed, with easy purchases from China, India, or domestic dealers. It only took a few clicks and a credit card to buy heroin, fentanyl, or any other drug on the open internet. Those sites were so obvious that most were shut down, but the sellers simply moved their products to the "dark web" or other channels in social media and sold even more. Counterfeit pills, heroin, and fentanyl were increasingly funneled by the millions through Mexico or Canada or through overnight delivery services and even the U.S. mail. Even as I saw the proliferation of online drug trafficking unfold, I still didn't check Macky's computer or phone. He could have easily gotten around anything I tried, but maybe I could have come up with *something* and at least he would have known I was trying to protect him.

Even as overdose deaths accelerated, I *still* didn't have Narcan around. I knew Narcan reversed most opioid overdoses in seconds, and I had given it a thousand times at work, but I didn't have a single dose at home if I ever needed it.

* * *

By 2016, opioids were both ubiquitous and cheap, available even in middle schools. Fentanyl had arrived and started to displace heroin and prescription opioids as it became the deadliest drug America had ever encountered. Macky was in recovery by then, but he was still at risk and knew every trick in the book about getting and using heroin if he wanted to. He could skip going to drug dealers and buy heroin, fentanyl, or anything else he wanted online and have it delivered to the front door.

He was deeply lonely with Emma being away at school. He faced the same difficulties anybody else his age had to cope with, but he had known drug use as his only pathway to relief. He was at high risk of relapse, but I didn't see it at the time. He knew more about street drugs than I did, so I didn't talk to him about the dangers of fentanyl. I didn't tell him to *never use alone* because I thought his drug use was behind him.

I never sat Macky down and told him that most people who die from an overdose are discovered at home, alone behind a closed door.

8

Accident

JUST BEFORE MIDNIGHT ON NOVEMBER 26, 2016, MACKY WAS driving home on Route 62 in Sterling, empty at that time of night. He was alone, probably going around the speed limit of fifty miles an hour. There weren't any streetlights. It was Thanksgiving weekend, and he had been shooting pool with friends in Clinton. I don't remember if he had worked that night.

Suddenly, a small car shot out from a little side road. There was a big house on the corner on the left with overgrown bushes in the yard, and neither Macky nor the other driver could see each other's headlights. The driver of the other car must not have seen the stop sign there or maybe zipped right through it thinking there was no reason to stop with no sign of traffic coming from the left in the middle of the night.

Macky didn't have time to hit his brakes before his car slammed into the other one. Both spun and slid in swirls before coming to a stop, with Macky's car up against a curb. I could tell when I saw the car later that he probably wasn't wearing his seat belt considering all the damage to the interior, which must have been caused by him being whipped around inside the car. He had smashed his face into the windshield and broke through the glass and struck his chest against the steering wheel hard enough to bend it out of shape even though the airbags deployed. He crawled out the shattered rear window and made it to the street. The three victims—Macky and the two occupants of the other car—were taken to different hospitals.

The EMTs took Macky to the nearest hospital, in Clinton. Shortly after he arrived at the ER he started to come around and feel the pain from his injuries, and they wanted to help him.

"No opioids!" Macky said, according to what they later told me.

"Why not? That's what you need."

"I was a heroin addict but I quit. Please, *no* opioids."

Macky was bleeding and bruised, with injuries to his face, chest, and arms. The ER found he had a fractured right hand, contused ribs, and multiple lacerations. They weren't sure if he had also suffered lung injuries from the steering wheel impact. Shards of glass were embedded in his face and scalp, and the doctor plucked out what he could find. Macky was dazed for a while but never lost consciousness, and the hospital didn't find any evidence of brain injury. After the doctor and nurses cleaned his wounds, they put a splint on his right hand and arm and observed him for a few hours. During the night, police came and interviewed Macky about what happened. They also asked the ER doctor if Macky had alcohol or drugs in his system, and they said no, his toxicology screen was negative. The police didn't cite Macky for anything.

It was almost daylight on Sunday, November 27, when he was discharged and for some reason he went to Patty's house in Sterling just a few miles away from the hospital. I don't know how he got there, but I think she picked him up. Maybe the hospital called Patty because his driver's license showed her address. Nobody contacted me during the night, and I didn't even know Macky was injured and at the hospital.

Patty called me later that morning.

"Did you know Macky was in an accident last night?"

"An accident? Is he alright? What happened? Where is he?" I asked.

"He's at my house. His car was totaled and he's got some injuries, but I'm not sure what. He wants you to come and get him."

I left immediately to get him. I held him close when I got there and couldn't stop myself from trying to smell if there was any alcohol on his breath, but there wasn't. I was so familiar with that telltale smell in car accident victims I treated in the ER that I could estimate their blood alcohol level before we got the reading back from the lab test. Macky's seemed like zero.

He was banged up and bandaged, with his right arm in a cast and sling. He looked like he had been up all night, but his speech was clear and calm so I didn't suspect a head injury—or any mind-altering drugs. He told me that the doctor referred him to see an orthopedic surgeon in a few weeks for follow-up for his broken hand, but he wasn't sure about what else they found.

I asked him about the accident.

"What happened, Macky?"

"I was coming back from Clinton and a car came out of nowhere, right in front of me."

"Were you able to slow down?"

"No. It was really fast. I just saw a car suddenly shoot out from nowhere and before I could say 'Fuck!' I smashed into it. My car was twirling around and I couldn't do anything. When it stopped, I climbed out a window because I thought it might explode or start burning. I just sat there in the road and then police and ambulances came."

"Why didn't you call me last night, buddy?"

"For one thing, I didn't have my phone. Also, I already had a bunch of accidents and I didn't want to tell you I had another one."

"Macky, you never have to worry about calling me. I love you. We can get a car fixed or find another one if we need to. If you ever get hurt again, will you promise to let me know? Maybe you'll see how it is one day when you become a dad. *Nothing* matters more to me than *you*."

I found out where the accident was and tried to figure out what happened by the tire streaks on the blacktop and the scattered pieces of glass, metal fragments, and red plastic the tow truck guys had missed. I drove down the street he was on and took some video of what he must have seen, then went down the little side street the other car was on. I went back and did the same thing late at night. It was easy to figure out how it probably happened, and when I got the police report later it looked like we reached the same conclusion. The other driver just didn't see Macky and pulled directly in front of him.

I went to the locked tow truck yard where his car was. I knew the mechanics at the station because I had been there so many times over the years, and they let me go in to retrieve his stuff. The car was totaled with the windows smashed, the steering wheel bent, and the seats ripped from the floor. Blood spattered the airbag and upholstery. I shuddered to think he was inside that the night before as I reached around picking up his belongings. Broken glass was strewn everywhere. I found some school papers and his backpack with a few books inside with pens and pencils and then saw his pool cue in the back. I looked closely for any drug paraphernalia—syringes, spoons, and even rolling papers—but there was nothing. There were no beer cans or liquor bottles. I took some pictures and left.

I went to the hospital and got a consent form for Macky to sign. After he signed it I went back and got his medical records and copies of the X-rays. I went over everything to see if I agreed with what they did and if there was anything suspicious about what happened, but there was nothing amiss.

The X-rays showed a hand fracture in a place doctors call "no-man's-land" because it is so easy to have something go wrong with injuries there. I called a hand surgeon I trusted and told him what I saw.

He said, "Jim, he needs an operation and soon. It shouldn't be hard to repair, but if we wait more than a week he could lose hand function. Is he right handed?"

"Yes. He's also a drummer and a writer."

"Well, whatever he does with his hands it's still something that can't wait. Can you bring him in tomorrow?"

I drove him to the surgeon's office in Worcester the next morning. Both of us dressed neatly, but Macky had trouble putting his clothes on because he could use only one hand and he wouldn't let me help him.

A nurse came out to get us.

"Maxwell Baker?" she said.

We both stood up to go with her, but Macky stopped me.

"I want to go in alone," he told me. "Can you just wait here, please?"

"Umm . . . I guess so. Do you need privacy?"

He just nodded and went in with the nurse.

Before long, the doctor came out to talk to me. He had the X-rays in his hand and showed me what he was concerned about and what kind of surgery Macky needed.

"He seems like a really good kid," he said. "He was straight with me, too. He told me about his heroin addiction history and his recovery. He said he didn't want any opioids, and he really insisted he was serious about that. I bet you're proud of him."

* * *

We scheduled the operation for seven in the morning on December 2, 2016.

Macky's pain was getting worse, especially in his chest. His hand didn't hurt because it was immobilized with a plaster splint, and he was careful moving around in his sling. He stuck to his guns about pain medicine and asked me how much Tylenol or Motrin he could take and if it would be alright if he took them at the same time.

Emma was still away for her semester abroad in Costa Rica, and Macky could talk to her only when she wasn't busy with class and had enough Wi-Fi service to use her phone. He had told her about the accident and upcoming surgery, but they couldn't linger long on the phone before the calls dropped. I talked with Emma, too, and gave her my opinions both as a doctor and as Macky's dad. I told her that I would let her know when the surgery was done and that Macky was okay.

The night before the operation, Macky couldn't take anything by mouth after midnight so that he would be safe for anesthesia. He didn't say anything about pain and didn't ask for medicine. He got up early.

"I just want to get this over with and use my hand again," he told me during our early morning drive to the outpatient surgery center.

"That should be pretty soon, buddy. You have a really good surgeon and I'm going to help afterwards. You'll be yourself again before you know it!"

* * *

We arrived well before seven and signed in. They had us sit in a waiting area, then a nurse in blue scrubs and a paper bonnet came out to get us. She slapped her hand on a metal plate on the wall and two heavy wooden doors opened. We walked into a brightly lit room with a linoleum floor and tiled walls. Stretchers lined the walls with curtains separating the patients. The room smelled like rubbing alcohol. Blue lights flashed vital sign readings on screens next to the patients as rhythmic chirps beeped with each heartbeat and squiggly yellow lines traced each patient's heart electrical activity.

The nurse handed Macky a speckled blue johnny.

"Go into the changing area and take everything off, okay? Put this on with the opening in back," she told him.

It took him a while but he got himself into the gown. When he got back to his stretcher, she looked at her clipboard and asked him the same questions we were about to hear over and over again.

"Name? Date of birth? Allergies? Here for hand surgery?"

He answered, and she clipped a plastic band around his wrist to identify him.

Everyone who talked to Macky asked him the same things even though they already knew the answers. All those things are written in the chart, but everyone needed to verify that they had the right patient and correct information rather than trust somebody else's notes. I knew that in today's medical world, every person who interacted with a patient had to verify they were caring for the right one and not just rely on someone else's note.

Throughout my career, I did the same thing. I thought about the thousands of chart entries I read that said "hx IVDA," which meant "history of intravenous drug abuse" and set the stage for mistrust and sometimes callous treatment. I didn't know if Macky's operating room records had that on it. I also thought Macky's decision to *not* receive opioids should have been in the chart but probably wasn't. Nobody asked him about it.

I smiled at him because I was happy to get this done and we joked a little. Both of us were somewhat scared about the operation even though the surgeon said it wasn't going to be a big deal. Macky was thrilled that his hand was about to be repaired.

I heard a female voice on the other side of the room. She said she was the new anesthesiologist and introduced herself to someone who must have been the charge nurse. I didn't catch the anesthesiologist's name. Whomever she was talking with welcomed her and I could hear them chatting.

I thought, "New? Does she know what she's doing? Is she fresh out of training and bristling with modern knowledge or is she still wet behind the ears?"

I didn't think Macky's anesthesia would be complicated for such a short procedure so I didn't worry. I had worked with anesthesiologists for years, especially during my internship in surgery. They always seemed gifted in their meticulous management of patients who needed the most potent and dangerous medications in all of medicine—drugs that temporarily paralyze the patient. They then put the patients deeply asleep and a step or two away from death. After every operation the anesthesiologist cautiously woke the patient up and protected each one from pain while soothing their fears.

"Where am I? What happened? Who are you?" patients would ask as the anesthesia wore off.

"Shhh . . . it's okay. You're at the hospital, you just had surgery. You're waking up now."

I saw anesthesiologists do that over and over. They had also helped me manage dire situations in the intensive care unit and the ER, and we made a good team.

But this doctor wasn't like that. She was impersonal and businesslike and seemed angry about something. I didn't know until later why.

* * *

The anesthesiologist wore hard-soled platform shoes that slapped loudly on the hard floor with every step. She walked up to Macky's bedside while I sat next to him on a small stool with a spinning seat. She was short with a slight frame and puffed out her chest by wearing an oversized surgical scrub jacket. I wondered why she had to make such a conspicuous entrance.

Her scrubs were rumpled, like she was signaling she was too busy or important to care about her appearance. She propped her paper bonnet on her head like a crown. An ID badge jangled from a chain around her neck along with a black stethoscope and a paper face mask with the strings askew. A variety of syringes and pens protruded from her chest pocket, and her scrub jacket pockets held laminated notecards like doctors in training use to help remember drug conversions or emergency procedures.

She leaned against Macky's bedrail, holding a clipboard.

"Name? Date of birth? Allergies? Here for hand surgery?" she asked in a robotic monotone, looking at his wristband while she spoke. "I'm the anesthesiologist," she said flatly. "I'm going to put you to sleep."

She listened to his heart and lungs, felt his abdomen, and examined the fingers of his right hand sticking out from the splint. She didn't speak to me or look in my direction.

She never smiled or offered reassurance. I didn't understand why she was so terse, but maybe she had been on call the night before for a hospital in town and had worked all night.

I thought, "Do I ever act like that to patients?" and realized maybe I did when I was tired or distracted and didn't consider how I was coming across. I know I was cold to my patients with heroin addiction after resuscitating them from overdoses. If they survived, they were angry and volatile, which triggered the same reaction in me unless I just didn't care to connect with them and just moved on to the next patient. Maybe she was exhausted. Maybe she didn't like former heroin addicts.

She put an IV line into his left arm, taped it in place, then said, "I'm going to give you something to help you relax."

She took two syringes from one of her coat pockets and injected whatever was in them into Macky's IV. She didn't say what the medications were, she didn't ask for his consent, and she didn't ask either of us if we had any concerns. It was not until much later that I found out that she knew that Macky had adamantly refused the use of opioids, and she found that out because Macky's surgeon had told her. If she had asked Macky, she would also have learned that he hated the effects of benzodiazepines and would never use them. Nevertheless, one syringe the anesthesiologist injected into Macky was fentanyl, a particularly powerful opioid, and the other was Versed (midazolam), an especially potent benzodiazepine. Macky closed his eyes within seconds.

The surgeon came over a little later. He wore scrubs like everybody else except his hat was a cloth bandana, like Japanese sushi chefs wear. He was tall, walked fast, and spoke confidently, like other surgeons I knew. He smiled warmly and shook my hand. He said, "Morning, Jim!" He looked down at Macky, now drowsy on the stretcher.

"Hey, Max—excited? Ready to get this done?" he asked.

"Yep," Macky murmured without opening his eyes. "Really ready."

"Alright, we'll have you in there soon. Should be easy," he said as he patted Macky on the shoulder.

Next, heavy doors on the other side of the room swung open and two women in medical garb came out from what appeared to be the operating room. They asked Macky the same questions again. One of them kicked the lock on the stretcher wheel and they rolled him away.

"I love you, Macky!" I called out to him.

* * *

I sat there by the curtain, alone with the monitors and medical equipment now disconnected from him while he was in the other room having his surgery.

I saw the anesthesiologist walking by and got her attention.

"Excuse me, Doctor. May I ask you something?"

"What?" she said, as she crossed her arms.

"I just wanted to ask if that was fentanyl and Versed you gave him." I knew those drugs were common both in the ER and in anesthesia, but I knew Macky didn't want them.

She uncrossed her arms and put her hands on her hips with her feet now spread apart, looking like a ship captain confronting an unruly crew. I could see her jaw muscles tighten before she answered.

"Yes," she said.

I thought she might follow with, "You got a problem with that?" but she didn't need to say it because I could see it in her eyes.

She then spun around and walked away with the same heavy, deliberate thumps in her steps that I heard earlier. I never saw her again.

I still didn't know why she seemed so brusque or if I was just imagining her attitude as confrontational. The surgeon told me several weeks later that he had told her about Macky's history of heroin addiction and recovery. He said he asked her not to use opioids because Macky had been so clear about his fear of relapse.

"Can we get this done without opioids? That's the one thing he asked and I don't want this to go wrong," the surgeon told me he had said.

"I don't care," she said. "There's no literature that says I need to manage him any different from the rest of my patients. I'm going to treat him the way I want."

And she did.

* * *

I went back out to the waiting room for a cup of coffee. I didn't think much about the anesthesiologist except to wonder if she chose that specialty because her patients were asleep with a paper drape between her and everybody else in the room. I didn't want to criticize a fellow medical professional just because she had a different bedside manner and a sharp edge to her care. Maybe she was usually a warm and gentle physician. I did my best to put aside the interaction I had with her and instead thought about Macky back there in the operating room, getting his hand repaired so he could continue his journey back to a normal life.

Shortly before nine, the doors in the waiting area swung open again and the surgeon appeared. He waved me over.

"How'd it go?" I asked.

"It was perfect—the screws went in nicely and everything is aligned again."

"Oh, doctor—thank you! Can I go see him now?" I asked as I started to walk past him.

He quickly reached up and swung his arm around my shoulder and firmly turned me around and back out the door.

"Wait a minute, Jim. There's a problem."

"A problem?" I asked. "Is he alright?"

"He's alright. The procedure went fine, but something changed in him. He's really pissed."

"About what? Does he know everything is fixed?"

"Yes, but he doesn't care about that. He's asking me for drugs. I don't know what happened. He said he had to have Percocet. He's like a completely different person all of a sudden and I . . . I . . . I just don't know what to *do*. God, this is horrible."

I knew Percocet was the brand name for the pills containing oxycodone, the same opioid in OxyContin, except Percocet contains the "immediate release" formulation. Both the surgeon and I knew that Macky made it clear before that he didn't want that.

I didn't understand why he was mad. The first day they met Macky had confessed to the surgeon that he was in recovery, and they agreed to keep Macky safe by staying away from opioids.

"I don't know what's going on, either. He told us he didn't want opioids. What happened?" I asked.

"I can't figure it out—I wasn't expecting this. It's really scary, Jim. What should we do?"

The surgeon rubbed his hand on his forehead and looked down, then up at me. I thought I saw mist in his eyes, but I wasn't sure.

I said, "I have to be his dad today. That's all I can think about."

His surgeon was trained to perform delicate operations and I didn't expect him to know how to handle this unexpected problem in pain management. But it wasn't just Macky's surgeon or me who didn't know what to do. Back then, *nobody* knew the right way to manage pain in patients recovering from addiction.

* * *

"Can you go talk to him about it?" the surgeon asked. "Maybe he'll listen to you."

A nurse took me back to Macky's stretcher. His right hand was in a big cast that went up his arm. He was awake, but his eyes were glazed and his eyelids drooped.

"Hey, buddy, you did it!" I said. "How are you feeling?"

"Not very good. I need drugs. Real drugs."

"But you said you didn't want those."

"I just had surgery and I *have* to get something."

"That could be a big problem for you, Macky. Your doctor is worried about you. Me too."

"Well, *I'm* not worried. I can handle it. Tell him I need Percocet, Dad."

The surgeon came over while I was talking with Macky and said, "I can't give you those, Max. It's not safe. You understand. If you really need something for pain, I could give you a prescription for a few Vicodin to get you through today. Are you alright with that?"

I knew Vicodin contained an opioid called hydrocodone. It isn't as powerful as oxycodone, but both are addictive opioids.

Macky was seething and wouldn't answer.

The surgeon wrote a prescription for six Vicodin tablets and gave it to Macky, who looked at the prescription and slapped it down on the gurney. He set his jaw, turned his head away, and blew out a slow breath.

I tried to change the mood.

"Hey, can we get a picture for Emma and let her know you're okay?" I asked.

He gave me a half smile to share with her but his eyes weren't right. He had that drugged look I remembered from his years of addiction.

"Let's go," he said. He didn't thank his doctor.

A nurse came over and told me to go get the car. She pulled the curtain closed to help him get dressed, then took him to the front door in a wheelchair.

He got in the car and was quiet at first, shifting around and looking repeatedly at his discharge papers and the prescription.

"I can't believe it," he said.

"Macky, you've worked hard for a long time. He's trying to protect you."

"Yeah, protect me. I need medicine, not 'protection.'"

Halfway home, he said, "Dad, can you call ahead to the pharmacy and tell them I'm coming? They can have it ready for me when we get there."

"No, that's not allowed. They'll get it ready pretty fast when we get there. I'll tell them you just had an operation."

"You can't do anything? You won't prescribe me some Percocet?"

"Hey, you know I can't do that."

Now he was mad at me, too.

We got to the pharmacy and only had to wait about fifteen minutes to get the prescription filled. The local pharmacist knew I was a doctor and always treated me nicely.

Macky wanted to hold the bag on the way back to our house, only a few blocks away. On the short ride home, he tore open the stapled brown bag, took out the little white bag with the pill bottle inside, and clutched it tightly.

We pulled into our driveway and he started to reach across his body with his left hand to grab the door handle before the car even stopped.

"Hey, hey—*careful*, Macky! You still have anesthetics in you," I said.

He jumped out of the car and moved fast to the back door as I ran to help him. We got inside and he went straight to the kitchen sink and ripped the bag open with his teeth. I couldn't see how he got the bottle cap off because it happened so quickly, but I think he grabbed the cap with his teeth and twisted it off. He took some pills out but I couldn't see how many. He shoved them into his mouth and turned on the water, drinking straight from the faucet to wash them down.

He said, "I'm going to lay down," and walked away without another word.

I stood in the kitchen thinking about what happened in less than ten seconds after we pulled into the driveway.

I went back through everything that happened that morning and who did what. Did I do something wrong? Did the surgeon make the right call in giving Macky pills to get him through his post-op day? Maybe he thought Macky would turn to the street again if he had untreated pain.

I believed we did the best we could. At the time, I was too rattled to see where the problem was. I didn't consider what probably triggered Macky's opioid receptors to light up again and suddenly cause him to crave more. I was too stunned by how things changed so suddenly and didn't even think about the fentanyl he was given. I was more concerned with what was going to happen next.

9

Danger

On Saturday, December 3, one day after his surgery, Macky walked into the kitchen a little wobbly. I didn't know if the anesthesia was still affecting him or if it was the Vicodin, but he wasn't himself. I made him some tea and gave him plastic cups of Jell-O.

"Don't worry about it, Macky," I said. "Everybody's woozy after an operation."

"I'm not worried, I just want to feel normal. Things are starting to hurt more."

"You were really banged up, and you feel it more after the first few days. Then after a week or two you start to get better. If you're done with that Vicodin, you can try Motrin or Tylenol. Chest injuries like yours take a long time to heal, but they still get better on their own."

"It's not a big deal. I just didn't expect to be in so much pain."

* * *

I had something to do in Boston that night so I took him to Patty's, where he stayed for two days. I picked him up on Monday, December 5. On the ride back to my house, I asked him how he was feeling and if he needed anything.

He said he was doing alright and then was quiet for a minute. He took in a deep breath and let it out slowly.

"I've been thinking about my life, Dad. I want to make some changes."

I looked over at him in the passenger's seat, his right arm in a sling and his left hand under his chin.

"Thinking about your life? That sounds pretty big. What's up?"

"I thought about the accident and how I could have been killed. And now I'm realizing I haven't accomplished anything. I'm like a nobody. I got off of heroin, but that doesn't matter to anybody except me. I got elected to the Student Senate, but all we did at the meetings was talk and never *did* anything. Politics isn't for me."

"Macky, you mention getting off heroin like it was nothing. Your recovery from that was the most important thing to me in the world. And you've still got your whole life ahead of you, buddy," I said. "So what are you thinking about doing?"

"I know a lot about addiction from the other side, and I bet I could help people. I want to be a doctor."

I was shocked—I never heard a word from him about that before.

"Wow, good for you!" I said. "You can accomplish whatever you want, Macky. That's your call. But you know what becoming a doctor takes, right? It's hard, man. Really hard. And it takes a long time just to get to square one."

"Yeah, I know. I watched you be a doctor my whole life, and I just saw what Cuff did."

She had just graduated medical school in June and then started her residency training at Massachusetts General Hospital the following week.

"So what do we do? How will you get started?" I asked.

"Will you take me to Lowell tomorrow so I can meet with my academic adviser? I can still change my major and reschedule all my courses for next term."

He called the school and made some appointments, and we drove to UMass Lowell the next day. We went from one office to another with me sitting in the halls waiting. Before one meeting, he casually pulled a piece of glass out of his face. "Look, Dad," he said, then threw the sliver into a trash can. The process took most of the day, but he eventually got all the approvals he needed to change his course schedule, paid some fees, and by that afternoon had his official letter in hand with classes lined up for his new pre-med major.

To celebrate, he wanted to go to a hot dog truck he knew in Lowell, so we did. We sat at a little metal table with folding chairs outside the truck with steam rising from our hot dogs and fries.

"Here we go, Dad. Wait 'til Emma hears."

He was beaming with pride with his new direction and couldn't wait to share the news with her. He wanted to compare his class schedule with hers so they could map out the next semester starting in another month or so.

* * *

Macky was still having problems with pain, and on the drive home he asked me if the doctors might have missed something. He told me his chest hurt when he took deep breaths or coughed, and he also kept getting headaches like he never felt before. The Motrin helped a little but not much. He asked me if I would find him a lung specialist or if I could arrange for more X-rays, maybe a CAT scan. I wasn't his doctor and wouldn't do that. I also didn't think he needed any more tests.

"I know it's scary to have these symptoms, but rib injuries are slow to heal and you need more time. And a serious blow to the head usually leads to headaches even when there isn't a detectable brain injury. You're going to get better."

He asked me if he might have suffered bruising to his lungs and I told him that even if that had happened it would get better with time and didn't need treatment. I found out later that he made an appointment with a pulmonologist on his own anyway and went to see him because a bill for the visit came weeks later.

He wanted to go to a neurologist about the headaches, but again I told him headaches were common after an accident, but as long as his thinking was clear and his coordination intact he should just give it some time. I suspect he went to a neurologist anyway and probably used Patty's health insurance because I didn't get a bill for that.

I started to worry when I received notifications for charges from my health plan from different pharmacies. I didn't know what medications he was getting, only the amounts charged for different dates at each pharmacy. I knew there was no effective treatment for either lung contusions or posttraumatic headaches other than pain management and time to recover, and I became queasy about what he was being prescribed without telling me.

He hated it when I investigated him or even poked around about his life, so I didn't ask if he was getting narcotics. He had visible injuries and recent surgery and was in a cast, so it would have been easy to get prescriptions. Macky knew how to behave with doctors and what to say to get pain medicines, so I knew he was at risk of going back to opioids. I watched for signs of opioid use but didn't see anything, like pinpoint pupils or slurred speech, but he had also learned ways to hide his opioid use around me, particularly by making himself scarce. He asked me questions about Naprosyn and Motrin, wanting to know how they were different and if they were safe for him. I didn't think about it at the time, but maybe he was just trying to make me think those non-opioid medicines were all he was taking. If he had gone back to opioids, he hid it well.

Macky also spent a lot more time with Homer at the house Homer bought in Worcester the previous summer. He got it for a song because it was so dilapidated, with no upkeep for decades and a broken washing machine sitting in the middle of the living room even when it was up for sale. Homer and Macky jumped headlong into cleanup and repair, and with hard, sweaty labor, they turned that house into a bit of a showcase.

Macky stayed with Homer often and helped him with grunt work that didn't require finesse or construction experience. He couldn't do anything to help after his accident, but they stayed close and Macky still tried to chip in by doing some painting with his left arm. He liked being with his brother or Emma a lot more than being with me, especially since he couldn't play his drums with his arm in a sling. His drum kit had been the main attraction to staying at my house. Staying with Homer also meant I couldn't watch him as closely as I wanted to, and he knew that.

* * *

On December 14, I drove Macky up to his surgeon's office in Leominster for a post-op visit. The doctor took off the cast, removed the stitches, and gently checked the function of Macky's hand.

"This looks really good, Max. I think we can get rid of this cast and put on a smaller splint. You can take it off for a while every day and start moving your fingers around. Sound good?"

"Yeah, that's great!" he said. "When can I start using it like normal? I want to start playing my drums."

"No way, Max. Not yet. That's too much impact at this stage. Give it a few more weeks," he said. "How are you doing otherwise?"

"My hand feels good, but I hurt all over the place. Especially my chest."

"You were pretty beat up, but you should be getting better soon. How are you doing with the meds?"

"Fine. Just Tylenol or Motrin. Whatever my dad says."

Having a light, removable splint thrilled Macky, and by the time we were in the car he was squeezing his hand into a light, careful fist and stretching out his fingers. He smiled at what he could do.

We stopped at a McDonald's just down the street from the doctor's office and went in for lunch. We talked over burgers and fries, and he reminded me that Emma was returning the next day, December 15, because her semester in Costa Rica was finally over. He told me that things in his life were really coming together. His hand was improving, school was starting soon with his new pre-med major, and, most important, Emma was coming home. He leaned forward over our little table and leaned sideways, smiling. "Can you believe it, Dad?"

Right after we left McDonald's, he told me to pull over in a parking lot across the street. He didn't say why. As soon as I stopped, he opened the car door, bent over, and threw up. He got back into the car without a word, then grabbed an old golf towel he saw on my back seat and wiped his mouth. His nonchalance about throwing up reminded me instantly of what I saw in Vietnam more than forty years earlier. On my first day in-country, I was standing in formation at Camp Alpha in Saigon, waiting for our sergeant. A soldier calmly stepped forward out of formation, walked up to a garbage can, bent over, and threw up in it. He wiped his mouth with the sleeve of his fatigues and got back in formation as though nothing happened. I saw other GIs do something similar when I arrived in Nha Trang a few days later. Soldiers stepped out of their hooch or turned from their gun positions and vomited, then went back to whatever they had been doing on the air base without a word. Nobody bent over and held their belly or moaned, and I didn't hear anyone say, "I'm sick."

I was a newbie in Vietnam, and I asked one of the other guys who had been in-country for a while, "How come people are barfing all the time. Is it the heat?"

He laughed.

"No, man. That's smack. Heroin. It makes you throw up. Ain't nothing—just happens."

Those blasé episodes of vomiting came to mind as soon as I saw Macky do the same thing in that parking lot that day. Everything was going fine—he looked happy and sounded good—but then he threw up and wiped his mouth when he got back into the car like it was nothing. I remembered those words I heard in Vietnam. "That's smack. Heroin. Ain't nothing."

"No, no, no," I thought. "Please don't let it be that."

* * *

The next day, Emma came back from Costa Rica after being gone since July. Macky was overjoyed on her return, and they started spending almost every day together. I hardly saw him except when they stopped by for a visit. If he was using drugs, prescribed or from the street, I couldn't tell because I didn't see him enough. I was uneasy about him saying he was in pain and the doctor visits he didn't tell me about—and the unsettling prescription charges.

At twenty-three, he could make his own medical decisions and I didn't want to violate his privacy or pry into his health matters even though at some level I understood that poor choices could threaten his life. I also thought that if he found out I was secretly investigating him, he would think I didn't trust him and then hide whatever he was doing and be even more at risk. That was my quandary.

I focused instead on his optimism and plans for the future. Macky told me he and Emma were looking for an apartment in

Lowell, and he also said he was getting together with Ryan, his bass player. Ryan had found a singer, and they would start playing again as soon as Macky could use his drumsticks. I wanted to believe that he was moving forward and that if he had slipped up along the way, he would get over it and back on track.

With the smaller splint on and wearing an Ace wrap bandage, he used his arm more. He was ready to drive again but didn't have a car anymore because of the accident. We looked for one that we could afford and that would get him safely up I-495 to Lowell and back again, as he could return to work soon. He said, "Whatever we get, I'm going to take good care of it, Dad. I'm not going to let it smell like pizza. I'll figure out something."

We found one for sale in Sterling and went to check it out. It was clean, the owner had records, and Macky liked how it was black and shiny. The seller turned out to be a friend of Casey's from high school, so she gave Macky a good deal. That was on Tuesday afternoon, December 20, the same day Patty left town to spend Christmas with her sister. She wouldn't be back until December 28, which I knew only because one of the boys told me about it. I didn't keep tabs on what she did or where she went.

The next morning, December 21, I got a cashier's check to pay for the car and told Macky it was a loan he could pay back some day. The seller's dad brought the car over, picked up the check, and left with the plates. Macky couldn't wait to register it and get back on the road.

Lots of things happened that day.

That's when he went to the pulmonologist without telling me and when he probably got a prescription for something.

The same morning, Anne drove out to a rural Christmas tree farm where the grower handed her a saw and said, "Find the one you want." She hiked down a snowy hill, picked out a tree, and cut it down herself, then dragged it back up and paid for it. The farmer tied it to the roof of her car, and when she got home I helped her put it up in the stand. Macky and Emma came over later to help put on the tree lights and decorations.

While they were decorating the tree, I was in another room reading the *New England Journal of Medicine* online. I paid special attention to an article by Surgeon General Vivek Murthy, titled "Ending the Opioid Epidemic—A Call to Action," an early release copy of an article to be published in the December 22 edition. Shortly after I read it, Macky, Emma, and Anne finished the tree and joined me in the front room. After a little chatting, I told Macky about what I just read and what the surgeon general recommended.

"You lived through addiction, Macky. You know a lot more about it than I do and probably more than most doctors, including the surgeon general. What do *you* think should be done?"

He said the surgeon general had good ideas, especially regarding physician education about addiction, but that was only one part of what could help.

He said the biggest problem was *stigma* because as long as people hated addicts, they wouldn't understand or help and instead would leave them isolated and stranded without hope. He told me most people with addiction want to come out of the shadows and rejoin their families and get back to school or work but were afraid of what would happen to them if people discovered their addiction. He asked again why doctors still didn't know *anything* about addiction or how to treat it. When people with addiction looked for medical help, there was almost nobody there to provide it, just as we found out when searching for help. He wanted to know why medical schools never taught the students about addiction. He asked me, "Is that because it's too hard to learn? Is it because the schools don't care? I don't understand why that happens. People with addiction are going to die unless they find effective treatment."

Macky admitted that his addiction was his own fault and that he alone was responsible for what he did. He asked if that decision to experiment with drugs should mean he would be denied medical care, even if the right treatment could save his life. He asked me what doctors thought about the thousands of overdose deaths happening every month and if they wanted to help. Was it because doctors believed that people with addiction deserved to die because addiction was the patient's own fault when they turned to drugs? Did doctors think that it was fair to see so many people die when they could have been helped?

He also asked why Narcan wasn't available everywhere when it could so easily save lives and was cheap and simple to use. He knew that most people who were revived would immediately go back to using because they were suddenly in withdrawal—but at least they would still be *alive* and have a chance to recover if someone cared enough to guide them to treatment.

I didn't know how to answer but I didn't want to accuse my physician colleagues of patient neglect or unethical behavior just because they didn't understand addiction. Doctors can't do things they are not trained to do and I respected that. I had never treated anybody for addiction either, except to resuscitate them if they were dying from an overdose or had a medical complication of some sort. I had to admit I was one of those doctors he was talking about. I didn't carry Narcan either or even know where to get it. And just like the general public, I had disdain for people with addiction. I didn't tell Macky what I was thinking—that he was correct that most of us in medicine believed that addiction really *was* a choice and that it was the patient's own fault for using. For a long time, I believed that they *wanted* to live like that and could have stopped anytime they wanted. I was too embarrassed to admit how wrong I had been.

I thought about my patients with illnesses that result from lifestyle choices like smoking or drinking. Physicians treated them for their lung cancer or liver cirrhosis no matter how much it cost or how complicated the care. I never heard any derogatory comments about the choices the patients made that led to their disease or why someone had a heart attack or stroke.

I remembered one night in the ER when I had two patients side by side in a large resuscitation room. One of them was a police officer, still in his uniform but covered in blood and dead on arrival from multiple gunshot wounds. Right next to the officer on another gurney was the person who shot him. He also had multiple gunshot wounds but was still alive, and nobody thought twice about doing all we could to save him so that's what we did. We didn't make judgments about who deserved medical care based on what decisions they had made or whatever they had done, no matter how awful. The only exception to that concept was caring for people with heroin addiction. We treated overdoses but not the underlying problem. Many medical professionals mirrored attitudes in the general public and said, "Just let them die—it's their own fault."

I didn't have the heart to share that with Macky that day, right after he had decorated our Christmas tree.

* * *

Even though it was December 21 instead of December 24, we decided to have our Christmas Eve that night. Emma needed to be with her family out in Framingham for the holiday, so we just made our own. Anne made a nice dinner, and afterward we gathered in the living room.

Macky built a fire using wood he had split in the backyard a month or two before the cold set in. Once the fireplace was going, we talked about our different plans for the New Year. Macky sat by the tree with Emma in his lap and they cuddled. He said we should play some music, so I brought out a small amp that had a microphone attached. We used it as a karaoke machine to play whatever music we wanted as we sang along. I decided it would be fun to play some rap music because I had learned the lyrics from a couple of movie soundtracks and it would be easy for me to just slam out the words rather than actually sing.

Macky looked disappointed when I started playing those songs and rapping into the microphone.

"Hey, Dad, um, do you think we could sing something else?"

"Like what?"

"How 'bout 'Rudolph the Red-Nosed Reindeer'?" he asked, "or 'Frosty the Snowman'?"

I didn't own any recordings like those, but I found some Bing Crosby versions of Christmas songs online, then hooked up a connection to the amp. As soon as the first song played, Macky and Emma looked at each other and started singing along. The light in the living room came from the glowing fire and the multicolored Christmas lights. The firewood crackled and the living room had the scent of a campfire mixed with the aroma of the fresh-cut tree. Bing crooned to the sounds of his 1950s orchestra and Anne and I joined in.

Later that night, after Anne and I had gone to bed, Macky and Emma left for Homer's. I didn't know when I would see them again.

* * *

Two days later, on December 23, our friends Phyllis and Dick from across the street hosted their annual Christmas party. All the neighbors were invited, along with family members. Anne and I got dressed up and went over. Casseroles, crockpots, and favorite family treats lined a big table, along with home-baked holiday desserts. There were bottles of wine for the adults and sodas for the kids. In a side room, Dick had set up a digital slide show on a big-screen television, and photos of almost everybody in the neighborhood cycled through. There were pictures from other get-togethers over the years, along with ones of little kids learning to ride their bikes or playing sports in the backyard. Dick was playing piano with songs like "Silent Night" and "Rocking Around the Christmas Tree" while partygoers sang along. I liked seeing everybody but wished I could see my own family.

Halfway through the night, I looked up from my chair and couldn't believe my eyes. Homer suddenly appeared in the group gathered in the kitchen, making his way through the crowd and holding his girlfriend Lauren's hand as she followed him. He was smiling and saying hello to everybody, shaking hands and embracing old friends. I got up and gave him a big hug and said, "Homes!" Then, right behind Homer and Lauren, Macky walked in, with his hair combed and dressed in a collared shirt and forest-green sweater. Emma followed him, holding his hand tightly and looking shy since she hardly knew anybody there. All I could say over the din was, "Macky! Emma!"

They made the rounds of saying hello to all the adults at the party—the parents who had spent years watching my boys grow up before Casey and Homer moved away to college—and Macky drifted off into his secret life. I tried to get some time with the boys and their girlfriends, but they were pulled in every direction and I settled for glimpses of them greeting everybody and laughing.

Neither Homer nor Macky had told me they were coming, and I didn't think they even knew the party was happening that night. They walked with confidence and spoke graciously, with warm and engaging manners. All the troubles Macky had lived through seemed to fade away that night.

* * *

On December 24, Macky made it to the motor vehicle registry with the papers he needed and received new license plates for his car. He smiled from ear to ear as he attached them in the dark later that evening and I snapped a picture. He and Emma had come over unexpectedly, but I should have anticipated that he wanted to get his car ready to put on the road. We were all in a festive mood, and Anne quickly put together a dinner with what we had on hand because we had no idea that anyone was even going to be coming over and hadn't done any food shopping. Macky called Homer and persuaded him and Lauren to come over, too. They arrived before long and we opened some presents together. I didn't stay up late because I was on call that weekend; my hospice was always busy on Christmas and my phone would be ringing all day. All the kids went back to Homer's later that night.

On Christmas Day, only Anne and I were at home in the morning. Macky came over a little later to see us and exchange the rest of our presents. I had decided to get him things for school and splurged on a new laptop and a few other items that cost more than I could really afford, but I knew he was serious about college now and I wanted to help. He looked surprised but uncomfortable when he opened the box with the computer. He didn't open the packaging any further to check it out or maybe fire it up. Instead, he put it aside and stacked it up with his other things. I didn't understand why he didn't seem happy about it.

Anne had told me she wanted some new kitchen things so I bought her a set of pots and pans from Sam's Club. She unwrapped the box and looked at it like I had just given her a Christmas present of vacuum cleaner bags. I didn't realize until later she was probably hoping for copper cookware from France instead of the stuff I bought for her. She was polite and said, "Oh. How nice."

She told me the next day that Macky was eyeing her box of new pans.

"Why would he care about those but not the new computer?" I asked.

"Because he and Emma are moving in together next week and making their first home," she said. "Remember?"

"But that computer was expensive, the best one I could find for him. I'm kind of hurt."

"Jim, he doesn't want to get things from you, especially something like that. You'll have to think about why."

* * *

By about two in the afternoon that day both Anne and Macky got ready to leave. Anne was going to her sister's house in Northampton for a day or two and would then go back to her place in Weston. We were still separated and lived in different homes in that unusual arrangement that seemed to work for us at the time. Macky packed some of his new things in his car and got ready to go be with Emma and her family at her grandmother's house for the rest of the holiday. He said he was going over to his mother's house after Christmas to see her and would be back in a few days. I was already on the phone answering calls from the nurses and it was fine with me to be alone the rest of the day.

Anne was dressed up in nice holiday clothes for her visit with her sister, and Macky got cleaned up and put on a dress shirt and sweater to visit Emma and her family. Both of them had their cars started at the same time in the driveway to warm them up before their long drives.

I sat in the front room on my phone, taking some notes while they scurried around getting ready. Anne came into the room where I was sitting. She reminded me about the details of her plans and started to say good-bye. Macky came in the room just then.

"Well, Dad, I gotta get going," he said.

I came over and hugged and kissed him, as I did every time one of my children entered or left the house.

"K—I love you, Macky," I said as I put my arms around him.

"Love you, too, Dad." He gave me a hug and a kiss, then turned toward Anne.

"I love you, Macky," Anne said as she squeezed him.

"I love you, Anne," he responded as he put his arms around her.

Running a little behind and anxious to see Emma, he turned around and left in a rush.

Anne smiled broadly and threw her hair back, then put her hands on her hips.

"Well!" she said. "Did you ever think we'd get to see him like *that* again?"

"Nope. But it sure makes me happy."

* * *

The next day, I was alone until Homer and Lauren stopped by again in the afternoon.

At one point, Homer was in the kitchen while Lauren and I sat together chatting. We talked about the party they had planned for the rest of the day. Lauren then looked around and said, "Where's Max?"

"In Sterling. He went to see his mother," I said.
"I thought she was in North Carolina with her sister."
We looked away from each other and my heart sank.

* * *

On Tuesday morning, December 27, Macky pawned my camera.

10

Terror

JUST BEFORE ONE O'CLOCK IN THE AFTERNOON OF WEDNESDAY, December 28, 2016, my phone rang. Homer's picture appeared.

I had gone to the Worcester Galleria to buy a present for Macky, a heavy-duty rope toy that he could use to play with our dog, Gronky, a rescue pit bull/lab mix who had chewed through the regular ones we tried. I had seen it a few days before, but it was expensive and I hoped the store might mark it down after Christmas. Somebody else beat me to it, though, and it was gone. I looked around for some sales, then went to the food court where I stood in line when the call came.

My eyes opened wide and I smiled when I saw it was Homer. He rarely called me in the middle of the day and I thought he might want to make some plans.

"Hey, Homes! What's up?"

His voice was low and serious. "Dad. Macky's unconscious."

"What? Unconscious?" I pictured Macky having taken too many pills again.

"Where is he?" I asked.

"He's at Mom's."

"I'm going over there right now," I said.

"Wait, Dad. There's an ambulance coming."

"An *ambulance*? What's going on? What's happening?"

"I don't know. I'm on way over there, too. Jon called me."

Jon had been Patty's boyfriend for a long time and they lived together.

I called him immediately. His voice quavered when he answered.

"Jon, this is Jim. What's going on with Macky?"

"I don't know. He's in the bathroom on the floor and I can't get the door open."

"Can you push it hard?"

"No. He's wedged up against it and I can only open it partway. I don't want to hurt him."

"Can you just break it down?" Jon was an older guy with a slight build, and I knew he couldn't knock a door off its hinges or kick it in the way the police do. I couldn't do that, either.

"I called 911, and they'll get it open somehow," he said.

I realized what might be happening and tried to rein in my terror.

"Jon, can you feel him?"

"Yes. I can get my hand in there."

I could tell Jon was in a panic and maybe more scared than I was. I didn't want to ask more questions, but I had to. I waited a few seconds before I continued.

"Is he breathing, Jon?"

"I . . . I . . . I can't tell," he said.

I took a long breath and paused again. I needed to ask an even tougher question, and I was terrified that I already knew the answer.

"Jon, is he cold?"

"Well, I just came in from outside," he said. "My hands are cold."

I didn't say anything.

"Okay, wait, I hear sirens. It's either the police or the ambulance. I have to go," he said, and hung up.

The drive from the mall in Worcester up to Sterling would take about twenty minutes even going as fast as I could without driving like a maniac. I pounded my fist on the steering wheel as I said out loud, "*Please* get the door open, use a hammer, bash it with your shoulder—push as hard as you can!" But then I pictured Jon encountering dead silence on the other side of Macky's bathroom door, then discovering Macky motionless on the floor. Jon had to be horrified. He wasn't a fireman, EMT, or cop and had never faced something like that before. I thought about what I would have done if I were there, that I would crash through that door however I had to. In reality, I couldn't rip any door down. I wouldn't have shoved it in as hard as I could, either—maybe Macky's head was up against it and I could have broken his neck. In the moment, I wanted Jon to *get inside and help him,* but he couldn't, not without an ax or sledgehammer. He told me he already called 911. What more could he do?

He had also told me he couldn't tell if Macky was breathing—and couldn't tell if the cold he felt was from his own hands or from Macky's body.

* * *

I tried to control myself but didn't do very well. My heart pounded and my throat was dry. I called Anne, but it went to voice mail. I called again and again, maybe forty times while I drove to Sterling. I just kept hitting redial and hearing the automated voice tell me to leave a message.

"Pick up, Anne. *Please* pick up!" I said to nobody. She would have answered if her phone were next to her all the time the way I always had my hospice phone with me. She had left it in her purse after the visit to her sister and didn't know I was calling.

In between those calls, I called Kerry, the nurse practitioner I worked with at my hospice agency, and told her that I thought something bad—really bad—was happening with my son and that I wouldn't be available for anything.

I called my neighbor Alice in Holden, a teenager who lived nearby and often took Gronky for walks, and asked her to take care of her. By then, I was in a panic, and I'm sure she could tell by my frightened voice and pleading tone that something was really wrong.

"Please, Alice, *please*. I think something horrible happened. I really need your help, Alice. Can you take care of her? Please?"

When she told me she would, her voice was high-pitched and her speech breathless, and I think she started to cry.

I don't remember whom else I called in that frantic state.

Macky was supposed to pick up Patty that afternoon in Providence, Rhode Island, after she flew home from her sister's that day. She waited at the airport and tried to call him, but there was no answer. I imagine she thought Macky forgot or hadn't charged his phone again. She must have been getting more and more aggravated as time went on, the way I would. "Where *is* he?" she must have thought.

Emma tried to reach Macky, too, and texted him that she wished he would keep his battery charged. She didn't have a clue about what was going on. Cuff was on her way back from a trip to Spain with her new husband, Sergio, and they were either still in the air or just arriving back to Boston. She couldn't know anything about what was happening. Casey was in Virginia, and I wasn't going to call him and tell him something so terrifying and have it turn out to be just a false alarm.

* * *

Before I made it to Patty's house, Homer called again, crying this time.

"Dad, it's too late. He's gone. Macky's dead." The words trickled out one at a time in between moans and gasps. He could barely speak.

"Are you *sure*, Homes?"

"They just told me, Dad." I could hardly make out his words, and I didn't want to believe what I thought he said.

"I'm almost there, Homes. Maybe there's something I can do," hoping against hope.

When I got closer to the house, I saw police cars everywhere, in the street and up the long driveway. There were black and white Sterling police cars, dark sedans with blacked-out windows and small antennas, and dark SUVs without any markings. None of them had their flashing lights on. There was no ambulance.

I walked to the side door, and before I went in I saw Homer through the window in the door. He sat at the kitchen table, hunched over, trembling, and crying out. Lauren stood over him stroking his hair and rubbing his back. When I opened the door, she looked up at me, then put her arms around Homer and held him as her red hair swung forward. As soon as I stepped in, I saw police officers walking slowly in the living room to my right. It looked like they didn't know what to say or do and seemed to avert their eyes from me, with one looking at a metal clipboard in his hands and another standing at the bottom of the stairs leading to Macky's bathroom and looking up at something. A third officer came up to me and said, "I'm sorry."

I didn't find out until much later how Homer learned his brother had died.

When he and Lauren had arrived outside Patty's house, Homer encountered an officer who must have already seen plenty of overdoses. Maybe he thought Homer was just another guy looking to make a buy from a dealer.

"Is everything alright with Max? How's he doing?" Homer had asked.

"That guy? He's dead."

He saw Homer's reaction and realized what he had just done and quickly walked away.

* * *

I went to Homer first and then turned to one of the police officers.

"Where is he?" I asked.

"He's up there," and he turned his head upward toward the second-floor bathroom right above us.

"Up there" was directly above where Homer sat in the kitchen, just a few feet below where Macky's body was lying on the floor.

I approached the officer standing at the bottom of the stairs.

"Can I see him? I'm his father."

"No," he said. "I'm sorry. It's still a crime scene until we know what happened. You wouldn't want to see him like that anyway." Maybe the officer was right, but in that moment I would have given anything to go upstairs and be with Macky.

I went back to Homer and tried to soothe him, but he was inconsolable.

I had to tell our family, so I stepped out of the kitchen onto the back porch and started calling. Because it was just a few days after Christmas and almost everybody was home for the week, people answered right away. I still hadn't been able to reach Anne, but that wasn't my first priority anymore.

I called Casey first because, just like Homer, he was Macky's big brother and loved him unconditionally. I could tell he was happy to hear me call him in Virginia.

"Hey, Dad!" he said.

"Hi, Casey. Hey, man—I'm really sorry, but I have to tell you something bad. Really bad. It's about Macky."

He was silent for a minute, then asked, "What do you mean? Is he okay?"

"No, Case. He overdosed today at Mom's and he died. Macky's dead. I wish I didn't have to tell you, but it's real, buddy. He's gone. I'm here at Mom's with Homer and Lauren right now. The police are here."

He breathed heavily into his phone.

"Fuck. God*damn* it, Dad. I'm coming home. I'll be there tonight."

I called Eric, my best friend ever since college. He had known all of my children since birth and had always been part of their lives. He and Macky were especially close, as they bonded first through literature and science, then music and sports. Eric was living in Boston when I first came to Massachusetts for residency training in emergency medicine, and he came out to Sterling often to spend time with me and my family. He showed them how to use the computer, first by teaching them very young children's video games like *Frogger* and *Load the Truck*. He taught them all how to play chess, which became a passionate interest to Macky. Eric also took the training wheels off their bikes once each had learned to pedal and let them learn to fall and just get back up, skinned knees or not. Eric was part of our family. Macky and I had just talked with Eric on speakerphone a couple of weeks earlier, but when they started discussing books I hadn't read I just listened to their banter and slid into the background. None of us could have known that would be our last conversation together.

Eric's phone rang a few times.

"Yeah?" he answered, his usual response when he saw it was me calling.

I told him what happened.

"Fuck. I'm coming down." If he said anything more, I don't remember what it was.

I called my family in California but didn't remember doing that until my sister told me later.

I had to tell Emma. She answered in her singsong happy voice, and I could tell she was relieved to finally hear back from Macky or me. She had been trying to reach him all day.

I told her, but she couldn't believe it.

"No. That's not right. Dead? Macky's *dead*? That can't be." Whatever else she said was lost in the haze.

Someone had told my daughter Cuff, but I didn't know who. I reached her while she was on her way back from the airport in Boston, but she was too stunned to talk and didn't seem able to believe what had happened.

Anne had found out Macky was dead before I could reach her. Eric had told her. I don't remember how we finally connected because so much was happening so fast.

"Anne . . ." I said, before I just went silent and couldn't speak.

"I already know. Eric told me. I'm on my way," she said. There was no panic in her voice, and I sensed her capacity to maintain her calm for everybody else caught in the sudden whirlwind of horror.

Patty was still at the airport in Providence waiting for Macky to pick her up. Jon called her from another room and told her.

She called me immediately after they spoke, screaming and frantic. Macky was in her house, lying dead on the bathroom floor, and she couldn't get home for hours.

"Don't let anybody touch him—he's my *son!* Did you hear me? Don't let anybody *touch* him!"

Jon drove to Providence to get Patty, at least a two-hour round-trip drive no matter how fast they drove.

Patty called me again and again, sometimes in complete disbelief and at other times furious that the police were there but she wasn't. I told her they had to be there, and as hard as it was to say, I had to let her know that more were on their way and the medical examiner was coming, too.

"Tell those cops to stay away from him. Don't let *anybody* near him. Do you hear me? He's not their son, he's *mine*. Don't let anybody touch him!" she screamed.

I had no control over anything the police did. They were there to help, but they didn't know if Macky had overdosed, had committed suicide, or might have been murdered. That would be decided by the state police detectives and the medical examiner's office. I knew the investigation would include a close examination of the death scene, gathering evidence, and taking crime scene photos. I knew the medical examiner team was going to take Macky's body to Boston for an autopsy and there was no way I could stop them or make them wait until Patty got home. Patty must have realized all those things were going to happen, but she was too shocked and bewildered to grasp the reality of it all. I tried to tell her, but she couldn't accept they were going to take him away before she could get home.

"I don't care *who* they are, I'm coming home right now. *Don't let anybody take him away!*" she repeated.

* * *

Sometime around five, a state police detective arrived. He spoke to the Sterling officers, then went upstairs. He came back down after a while and said that he was sorry and that he had to interview me. We sat at Patty's dining room table. I don't remember much of the discussion except that the detective was kind and spoke gently to me. It didn't feel like any kind of an interrogation, even if in some ways it was.

The detective, Robert Parr, asked for everybody's names, dates of birth, the date and details of Macky's car accident, what went on over the last several days, and when we had last seen Macky. After filling out a stack of forms, he asked me, "Did the deceased have a drug problem?"

I was taken aback by him calling Macky "the deceased," even though by that time what he said was accurate. I just hadn't accepted it yet.

"Sir, I know you have to ask these questions and this is part of it," I said. "But it's not real to me yet. It's hard to hear you say 'the deceased.' He has a name, and it's Macky. Is that fair to ask? Please?"

I knew he wasn't there to be a grief counselor. He was a state police detective in my house to investigate the sudden, unattended death of a twenty-three-year-old who had evidence of trauma to his body. He wasn't there to hold my hand. He needed facts.

Nevertheless, he stopped his questioning for a moment. He looked me in the eye and in a much softer voice said, "I'm sorry, doctor. I understand. Did Macky have a drug problem?"

"Yes, heroin. But I thought he was over it."

* * *

The medical examiner van arrived, and two uniformed people, a male and a female, went upstairs with a suitcase of equipment to examine the death scene, collect more evidence, and take additional photographs. It was dark by then, and most of the police had departed. I knew the next step was for the medical examiner team to bring a folding metal tray upstairs to get Macky's body. I didn't want to see that so I went out the back door with Homer and Lauren to drive around the block until that part was over. After I went down the porch steps by the back door in the dark, I tripped over the aluminum body tray they had taken from their van at some point. The metal stretcher was lying flat in the driveway and I didn't see it.

Homer, Lauren, Anne, and I pulled around the block and waited, but we didn't realize we were facing down the street where the van was about to drive. After a little while, the white van with blacked-out rear windows made the turn and went off into the darkness.

"There he goes, Dad," Homer said.

"Bye, Macky," I said. "I love you, buddy."

We went back to the house and waited for Patty. With almost all the police now gone, I went to the bottom of the stairs and looked up for a moment before ascending. The bathroom door was leaning against a wall, the hinges splintered by what must have been a fireman's ax. I realized I hadn't gone up those stairs since I left almost twenty years earlier. As soon as I saw the bathroom light illuminating the stairs a memory came immediately to mind.

When Macky was a baby, Patty used to give him baths in a little blue plastic tub she put in the bathroom sink. One sunny afternoon, I watched from the stairway below while he squiggled and kicked in the water, and she sang to him:

"Nice and clean,
Nice and clean,
Now we're gonna be
All nice and clean."

Instead of encountering the smell of baby soap and the sight of fluffy towels from so long before, I came upon Macky's wallet on the sink, open to his color picture on his driver's license. The floor was littered with rumpled swaths of white gauze and plastic wrappers used to keep medical items sterile, something I was used to seeing after we performed resuscitations in the ER. There were splotches of blood and other stains on the floor and in the sink. I didn't go through his wallet or touch anything else because it seemed both unreal and somehow sacred.

I walked over to where I thought his bedroom was and looked around. It wasn't my house anymore so I didn't handle anything in there, either, except to look at a book lying open by the side of his bed. He loved classic novels and I wondered if he had been reading something like James Joyce or Dostoevsky. Instead, I saw the pages he had open were instructions on how to iron a shirt. I flipped over to the cover and saw that it was like a 1950s-era cookbook, with a smiling dad wearing a tie and standing next to his wife and kids looking happily up at him. Instead of a book of recipes, it was an old-fashioned guidebook about how to raise a family.

I put it back down.

A policeman came up the stairs and saw me go back into the bathroom again. He was about to leave but stopped and gave me a business card. He said, "I don't know, but maybe you'll want to call these people."

The card was for a company that did death scene cleanup services.

* * *

By nightfall, our family gathered at Homer's house in Worcester. Eric was there. I think Emma's parents drove her out. Cuff arrived with her husband, Sergio, and he ordered takeout for all of us. He was kind to everybody, hugging each of us tightly. Nobody could eat. We sat in a circle in the living room and tried to say comforting things to one another, but it was too raw for anything to catch. I tried to say something or other reminiscent of beautiful things Macky said or did, but it wasn't time for that yet. At some level, we all knew that this was our new life and that things would never be the same.

I knew word would get out fast to our friends and neighbors and to everybody who knew Macky. Anne and I left for Holden, and Eric came with us. I had never written an obituary, but I had to that night. I told the truth so that people could understand what can happen with addiction.

The same night, December 28, I realized I hadn't told Ryan. He and Macky had gotten back together with plans of reviving their music. The two of them had weathered the worst of Macky's storms but stayed tight through it all. Ryan knew Macky's problems, but like Homer, he never turned away. It was late when I called, and his father answered the phone with the tentative voice people use when they get a late-night call.

"Hello?"

"Who is that?" I heard his wife whisper in the background.

"This is Jim Baker, Macky's dad. I'm sorry to call so late, but can I talk to Ryan please? It's important."

There was silence for a few seconds as Ryan's mom asked, "Who's calling? *What's going on?*"

In a muffled tone, I heard him tell her, "It's Macky's dad."

"He's not here right now, Jim. Is everything okay?" he asked.

"No. It's bad news. The worst. Macky died today."

Ryan's mom shrieked in the background, "No, *no!*"

I told him I was sorry I had to call like that, but I knew Ryan needed to know.

I also called the pizzeria where Macky worked, even though it was already after ten and I thought they would be closed. I had never spoken with anybody there before, but somebody answered and I told him I was Max's dad and had to tell him Macky was dead. Even though he didn't know me, he could tell by my voice the story was true.

There were more people I had to call the next day, including the surgeon.

"What? What? *Dead?*" he said. "Oh my God, Jim. What happened? He was doing so well. I can't believe it . . . I don't know what to say. . . oh my God!"

I can't remember all the other calls I had to make or whom I spoke with, but I had to get started on funeral arrangements. There was a funeral home a few blocks from my house, and I had worked with the owner for years because he helped me with so many of my hospice patients' families after death. I'd been over there many times to complete death certificates and other arrangements, so I knew him and the rest of the staff as friends. When I first called, whoever answered said, "Hey, Dr. Baker. Good to hear from you!"

Then I told them what happened and the tone changed immediately. I walked over and we started going over the details of what I had to do. I couldn't bear to go down to the basement of the funeral parlor to choose a coffin. Again, I asked Anne and Patty if they could go over there later and find one that was really nice wood. Macky was an expert on different woods, grains, and natural hues from his years of drumming, so I wanted him to have a lovely wooden coffin.

* * *

I found a church in Sterling and didn't realize at the time it was the same one that Macky went to for meetings when he was a Cub Scout, wearing his bright-blue uniform. The church was also right next door to the library where the boys and I had spent so many hours in the children's section. The reverend spoke softly and kindly. She asked me to bring in Anne and Patty the next day. We talked about Macky, his life, and what was important to him. Before we went in to meet with her, I asked Macky's closest friends to share small stories and some words that would help provide insight into who he really was. I gave the list to the reverend.

I couldn't bring myself to find a grave site, so Anne and Patty worked together on that, too. I asked them if they could find somewhere peaceful and maybe under a tree. They found one in just one day, located in Sterling. I knew the area because that's where Macky learned to play T-ball. We had driven there when he was four or five, and to get to the field we had to drive right through the cemetery on a narrow lane. We looked at the tombstones and crosses, and I said, "Can you believe this, Macky? A *graveyard* at the ball field?"

* * *

Because Macky died just after Christmas, the state medical examiner's investigation into the manner and cause of his death took longer than usual. For days, Macky was in a refrigerator somewhere in the medical examiner's office in Boston. I knew a few people there because of all the deaths I had to report over the years and thought they might listen to some concerns I had. Because I had helped with performing autopsies at a hospital pathology lab when I was a college student, I knew how thorough those examinations were—and how totally impersonal. The pathologists looked for precise answers, and they examined the entire body, inside and out, with no emotion that I could detect. I didn't want to picture that happening to Macky.

I couldn't stop picturing him lying on an autopsy tray with a team of technicians wearing aprons with trays of steel instruments set up for the exam, and I knew everything that was probably going to happen. Instead of understanding his autopsy as a necessary clinical process, I thought of it as gruesome. I called one of the chief investigators I knew and asked if they could do a limited autopsy, which sometimes happened if the cause of death was obvious. I told him the police said Macky's death looked like a drug overdose and asked if maybe they could do a more limited exam. The investigator I spoke with understood my concern, but the message that made it through to the exam room pathologist must have been different from what I had hoped.

I received a call two days later from the pathologist who was preparing to perform the autopsy on Macky.

"This is the ME's office. I'm going to examine Maxwell Baker," a woman said. In the background, I heard echoes from the tiled walls, steel tables, and heavy drawers. Metal pans clanged, the ones used for weighing organs once they've been removed. With thousands of overdoses every year in Massachusetts, I could understand that another examination of a young person wasn't going to be anything special. The Massachusetts medical examiner's office probably did five or ten overdose autopsies *every day*, and Macky was probably just another one to them, no matter how much he meant to me.

"Thank you for calling, doctor," I said. "Is there anything you need to know from me that would help?"

"Yes," she said. "You the father?"

I thought the cause might be obvious, but I knew Macky still had visible trauma from his accident a few weeks earlier. I knew that those signs of injury would be a concern, but they had found a freshly used needle and what was probably heroin in the bathroom with him. I was hopeful they could do a more limited exam.

"I heard you don't want an autopsy. Why not?"

"No, no, that's not what I meant. It's just that I know about autopsies because I'm a doctor, too. I was just hoping you wouldn't have to do . . . all those things. It's hard for me to think about."

"Yeah, well, we're going to do an autopsy," she said, and hung up.

She was just doing her job and had to move along. For all she knew, maybe somebody murdered Macky. I was the one who asked for a limited autopsy so maybe she thought I killed him. There was nothing I could do but accept that they were doing what they had to do. I tried not to think about it.

* * *

Back on the evening of December 28, I had sent a note to my neighbors saying that Macky had died that day. My close friends Joe and his wife Nicole walked over from across the street, opened our front door, and without a word came to Anne and me and took turns holding us.

Three days later, on New Year's Eve, I saw Joe again, this time doing something on my front porch. I wondered if he had dropped off flowers. Eric and I were sitting in the front room and were trying to get some gentle conversation going, but nothing came out except broken sentences that trailed off into tears.

I made a cup of tea, "Tension Tamer," the herbal tea that Macky and I always took turns making for one another.

"Want some tea, Dad?" he would ask.

"That would be nice, Macky." It didn't matter if I just had coffee or had to get going for work, my answer was always yes.

"What kind?" he would ask, even though he knew what I was going to say.

"Do we have any Tension Tamer?" I asked, knowing there was always some in the cupboard and maybe a backup box just in case. Before I even answered, he had already put the little bag in my favorite cup.

Eric and I stayed in the front room as the sun went down.

Joe came to the door and asked me if I could come outside. Eric came with me, and as we got outside, Alice, the same neighborhood teenager I had called during my frantic ride to Patty's house the day

Macky died, took my hand and walked me to the front yard. A large group of my neighbors were gathered in the snow, some holding their little children wrapped in blankets.

I didn't know what I was seeing at first but then noticed my front porch was lined with flickering electric lights, like candles burning, that were placed in little colored bags spaced a few feet apart. The line of lights led down both sides of the driveway all the way to the street. Alice took me to the street and had me look down, and as far as I could see both sides of the street were lined with rows of those multicolored lights. She took me in the other direction and lights lined the street that way, too.

In the middle of my snow-covered yard where everyone had gathered there was a giant heart made of more candles reflecting off the snow. I made my way to the heart where my neighbors walked up and embraced me. I tried to speak and thank them, but the only thing I could do was cry.

Alice took charge of that heart through the entire winter, keeping the lights fresh and the heart glowing every night.

* * *

By January 4, Macky was back at the funeral home near my house. That evening, I was invited by the funeral director to come over for a "viewing," something I had never done before. I didn't want that finality because it was going to make things too real, but I did my best to steel my nerves and went to see him. Macky was lying in an open coffin, wearing a blue UMass Medical School sweatshirt because his sister had graduated from there a few months earlier and he hoped he might one day apply for admission there. Maybe one day he might have become a doctor, but I realized that this was the only way he would ever be able to wear that sweatshirt. This was as close as he would ever get to his dream.

I hadn't seen him since Christmas Day when I told him I loved him and he said, "I love you, too, Dad." I was just like all the other families I had tried to console through all those years in the ER when I had to talk to families after a sudden death. My mouth was dry, I trembled, and I couldn't stop my tears. Even seeing him there still and silent, I had trouble believing it was true. I can't remember what I said to him in his coffin with his eyes closed, but I remember telling him I would always love him. A part of me still hoped he somehow would open his eyes and tell me he was okay and not to worry.

Emma came to the funeral home that night, too, and went in to talk to him alone.

Homer and Lauren came with us, and Homer wanted privacy with his little brother/best friend to share what was in his heart. I never asked any of them what they said, and after a while we walked back to my house, knowing that Macky's life was truly over.

* * *

The next evening was the wake. I'd never been part of one and didn't know what to expect. Macky's coffin was in the front of a large room with rows of seats. Along the walls leading from the entrance and up to the coffin, we had placed some of his favorite things on tables set up along what would be the waiting line, and we put up pictures of him growing up through the years. His books were out, as were his pool cue, a baseball, a chess set, and that handmade poster, "The Timeline of My Life," from the second grade. A screen at the back of the room slowly cycled through pictures of our family together and joyous moments in Macky's life, with the gentle song "Buck Dancer's Choice" by Taj Mahal in the background.

I had set up speakers behind his coffin, now closed, where I stood with Emma, Anne, Cuff, Casey, Homer, Lauren, Patty, and

Jon. I knew Macky's favorite songs and played them just loud enough to feel the drums and bass because I thought Macky would have wanted that. We greeted everybody while about twenty songs cycled through several times, including the live version of "In Memory of Elizabeth Reed" by the Allman Brothers, one of the first songs Macky and I ever learned to play together. Everything was strange to me at the time, like I was watching it from afar and it wasn't real. I didn't even know who was there after a while as I started to feel as though I were in a different world somehow. There were hundreds and hundreds of people, and I felt myself wonder why everybody was so sad, crying and shaking as they came up.

The funeral was the next morning. The funeral home had put Macky into a new suit I went out and got for him, and inside there with him were secret mementos that each one of us who had seen him at the viewing had placed there when nobody was watching.

His shiny black drums were set up on the stage. The minister spoke about him and shared many of the stories and insights our friends and family had provided. The music therapist from my hospice serenaded us and played a song Emma told us Macky had been trying to learn for her and an acoustic version of "Blue Sky" for me, my favorite song. She sang "Ave Maria" for Patty.

One by one, family members stepped behind Macky's coffin and did their best to maintain their composure as they offered a remembrance and a good-bye.

I was the last. I remembered attending a funeral of a child who was struck by a car and killed in Sterling, just up the street from my house. He was a classmate of Homer's and we went to the funeral. I remember thinking that if one of my children died suddenly, I wouldn't be able to draw another breath—or want to. But that child's father stood up next to his son's casket and slowly thanked everybody for coming and sharing their kindness. That was one of the bravest things I ever saw, and I thought to myself that I could never do that. But when my time came, it wasn't bravery. It was love, and I wanted to do it. I don't remember what I said except to quote Elizabeth Barrett Browning.

"How do I love thee? Let me count the ways."

* * *

When Macky developed addiction, there were only two possible outcomes: recovery or death. I should have understood that grim reality and then done whatever I had to in order to help him recover. Continued care with appropriate medications offered him the best option for recovery, and that is also true for others with opioid addiction. He didn't have to die.

I didn't know about medical treatment and thought I could force him to quit by threatening him, shaming him, or battering his emotions. Those actions made his addiction *worse* as he sought solace in the only method he knew: by using more drugs.

There were also times when I treated him with kindness and understanding. That's when he responded with cooperation and agreed to try to stop; even though the methods we tried were complete failures, at least I discovered that the most critical element in helping was compassion instead of cruelty. If I had sustained my understanding and care, then he would have had a chance to recover.

Most of the doctors who refused to help Macky turned him away because they didn't know what to do, but that wasn't their fault and I couldn't blame them. I didn't know what to do at that time, either.

We learned about interventions that didn't work, but I should have made more of an effort to learn about what kinds of treatment *do* work based on science instead of advertisements, myth, or convenience. Then I could have searched for the kind of care he needed.

It was only after he died that I began to accept that genetics and adverse childhood experiences are the most powerful predictors of addiction. His genetic predisposition couldn't change, but the adverse childhood experiences he faced should never have happened. He didn't suffer sexual or physical abuse, but he definitely lived through emotional torment that persisted throughout his childhood. I should have resolved my perpetual conflicts with Patty and then managed my own angry behaviors.

* * *

I didn't learn what I should have learned while Macky was still alive. Now, instead of watching him cultivate his budding relationship with Emma and work toward his goal of helping others, I visit his grave and leave him some of his favorite snacks, like kiwi fruit and sunflower seeds. Sometimes I bring him pictures of Emma or a cup of "Tension Tamer" tea.

I kiss the cold ground and say, "I love you, Macky."

11

Onward

"I observed the decedent lying face down in the bathroom. He was wearing a black t-shirt, jeans, and socks. Next to the decedent was a capped needle, alcohol swabs, q-tips, and an empty plastic bag." Massachusetts State Police Homicide/Death Report, December 28, 2016

* * *

After Macky's death on December 28, 2016, I learned about grief in ways I never anticipated. I had been present for thousands of deaths, either sudden and unexpected in the ER or inevitable from terminal illness in hospice care. I had witnessed families suffer their losses in a wide-ranging swath of sorrow, and I thought I would be ready if I ever had to face death in my own family. I was wrong.

I had last seen Macky all cleaned up, happy, and excited to go see Emma when he left my house on Christmas morning. Three days later, I was being questioned by the state police at Patty's house while his body was still on the bathroom floor above where we sat. A few hours later, after the medical examiner had taken him away for the autopsy, I had joined the rest of my family at Homer's house to console one another as best we could.

Patty sank deep into the cushions of Homer's couch and held one arm against her eyes as she tilted her head from side to side, moaning and trembling with tears streaming down her cheeks.

Emma sat up straight and seemed to peer into the distance, expressionless and silent as though she were in a trance. Homer cuddled quietly with Lauren, who softly stroked his hair. Casey sat near Patty and looked vacantly up toward the ceiling. Cuff tilted her head forward with her eyes closed and her fingers spread across her forehead as she slowly rocked back and forth. Sergio went to Cuff and rubbed her back and got up every few minutes to put take-out food onto plates and serve each of us things that none of us could eat. Anne looked around at everyone in the room as though she were assessing what she could do to somehow soothe the pain. Eric sat alone in a darkened corner.

To me, Macky's death still wasn't real yet, but my family's agony was right in front of me in every direction. I tried to bring lightness into the room.

"Do you guys remember the time when Macky won the tractor pull and how happy he was with that trophy?" I said.

"Nobody is ready for that kind of talk," Cuff said.

Silence followed, except for the sounds of sobs, whimpers, and moans. Sergio's Spanish voice, usually exuberant and excitable, changed to a warm and soft pitch as though he were comforting an injured child.

I could hardly think about everything I had to do, but I knew the first thing was to compose that obituary. I didn't want friends and neighbors finding out by word of mouth: "Did you hear about Macky Baker?" We had work to do, no matter how painful it was going to be. Taking on those responsibilities protected me from dwelling in my own despair, at least for a while.

I wrote the obituary that night, without the luxury of time or the freedom to think back through his life. I sent what I wrote to the funeral director, but I hadn't considered that the rest of my family had thoughts, too, and they wanted to share them. Very quickly,

I had to combine the different versions to respect how each of us felt, and the obituary came out as an amalgam that seemed to veer in different directions. The way the words were written hardly mattered, though, because the most important message to share was that Macky was dead and that the cause was an overdose following his long battle with addiction.

* * *

Right after he died, I started to wake up in the morning trembling from what I thought was a nightmare. I shuddered on awakening but then felt glad it was only a dream and Macky was really okay, still snuggled in his room, but then I remembered it wasn't a nightmare. I had to rediscover his death was real.

In the months that followed, tears flowed without warning. In the middle of conversations or performing mundane tasks, I sometimes found myself crying uncontrollably and unable to finish a sentence or cook an egg. There were times I had to stop driving, pull over, and wait because I couldn't see. I still brewed cups of the tea Macky and I used enjoy together, but I just gazed at the swirls of steam and savored the scent of peppermint and ginger. I didn't want to drink it alone.

Eventually, I came to recognize that the heartache I believed was unique to me was actually universal for every parent who has lost a child. I started to feel connected to other families who had to carry on after a devastating loss.

There were times after his death that I didn't want to go on and believed that, like Prometheus, my destiny would be eternal suffering unless I joined Macky in death. I understood why parents chose to end their suffering after losing a child, either by killing themselves, drinking, hiding under their blankets, or any other avenue that might free them from their pain. I shared those thoughts with a psychiatrist and he guided me back to rational thinking and hope.

"Macky wouldn't want you to do that, Jim," he said. "Your other children need you and love you. Anne loves you, too. Think about what Macky would tell you if he could."

A close friend I had known for many years said, "Jim, please don't bury yourself along with Macky."

I decided to just do my best to get from one day to the next and accept the kindness offered to me by neighbors who brought food and companionship, and friends and family who listened patiently to me as I talked and cried.

* * *

Months later, I took Gronky out for another walk around the block. I had been living in constant gloom throughout the winter, reliving the events of Macky's life and death and ruminating about what I should have done differently and how much life had changed since December 28.

It was May then, and the long New England winter of snow and ice had ended. The days were getting longer, the weather had turned warm, and green buds appeared on the trees. I felt the sunshine on my face as I looked up through the trees and between their slender branches silhouetted against the blue sky. Gronky was sniffing around the fragrant grass and tugging on her leash to explore the scents.

A feeling alighted in me that I didn't recognize for a moment, until I realized that what I felt was a twinge of happiness. I thought that emotion was gone from me forever and tingled with delight that somehow, even for a moment, it returned. All it took was a walk around the block with Gronky in the morning sunshine.

As I went along, I could sense Macky's warm voice as though he were walking alongside me but somehow above in the brilliant sky.

"Dad, this is how I want you to feel—happy," he said. "I'm gone now, but you need to go on. There are things you can do, even if that's just feeling glad to be alive. I know you are hurt and that's natural. But I told you some things you could do for other people with addiction and I hope you can do them."

I laughed with joy to feel his presence, but I cried at the same time. I was a mess of mussed-up hair with a face full of tears by the time Gronky and I made it around the block. During that short walk, I discovered that Macky and I were still connected through ways I might never understand. However his words came to me was a mystery I didn't understand, but what mattered more to me right then was to honor his wishes. I wanted to cultivate the joy I felt from feeling that he was still with me and that we didn't need to be playing catch or jamming in the basement to be together. And I wanted to get to work on making a difference.

* * *

I had already started studying addiction and learning about different treatments but wasn't sure what to do with that knowledge. I studied every resource I could find, especially from high-quality medical literature based on the work of scientists at major teaching hospitals. But that wasn't enough so I started investigating addiction out in the real world.

I went out with the police in Worcester, accompanying a team of officers who responded to overdoses and met with survivors and families to offer support. We visited homeless shelters, encampments, and treatment centers. The people with addiction we met knew and trusted the officers, and family members appreciated their kindness. Those officers knew that most people suffering with addiction would quit if they could only find help. The officers I met were compassionate and caring and knew how to relate to the people on the street. I had encountered the same attitude when Macky was alive, as police tried to help me get him help before it was too late.

I visited a large ER in Worcester and met with leadership and staff. I was board certified in emergency medicine and offered to help in the care of people with addiction as a volunteer doctor. I think that was a jarring notion at the time and they told me they had things under control. I was also still in a whirlwind of grief and I think they saw that I needed more time to recover.

I traveled to New York and visited a sober home there. The man who ran it, Jimmy, was in recovery himself and knew the hard life and crafty schemes of addiction and the importance of having someone care in order to recover. He accompanied people going to meetings at any hour and was always available to provide guidance himself, and I could see that he genuinely cared. That's not how most sober homes work because they can be easily turned into unlicensed, for-profit facilities that are a haven for continued drug use. Jimmy expected the people staying with him to remain sober and he couldn't be fooled.

In Los Angeles, I visited with police chiefs and public health officials as they looked for ways to address the rapidly worsening problem of addiction and death. They knew that treatment was the best answer and that incarceration did not help. Even so, a large portion of their jail inmate population had committed drug-related crimes, so the Los Angeles County jail, the largest prison in the world, started a drug treatment unit so that on release there was at least a chance that recovery would continue. The officers invited me into the prison to show me how their treatment system functioned and to meet face-to-face with prisoners who told me how they got there and how they hoped to improve with medical care.

In rural Massachusetts, I spent a day with a family practice doctor, Dr. Steve Martin, who treated people with heroin addiction right from his rural office in a town called Barre. He knew all about Suboxone and how to prescribe it but also maintained connections with addiction experts for complicated issues. He asked me if I wanted to see how he did it, and the patient consented.

The nurse had called the patient from the waiting room where others sat waiting for their physicals or whatever else took them to the doctor.

"Joe?" she called, and he came into the treatment area.

Joe and Dr. Martin greeted each other warmly and talked about how things were going, where Joe was living, and if he was working. The doctor asked if Joe had any cravings or was tempted to use again. Joe gave urine for a toxicology screen to show he wasn't using. He didn't need any adjustment to his Suboxone and was scheduled to come back in a couple of weeks.

"Isn't that amazing to see?" Dr. Martin asked.

I found out that some of the most knowledgeable addiction experts in the world were right nearby in Boston, so I went to meet them to learn even more. Dr. Sarah Wakeman, a brilliant and esteemed addiction researcher at Harvard Medical School, welcomed me with open arms. She knew what happened and offered me kindness and a sincere promise to help me if there was anything I needed.

Dr. Wakeman directed the Substance Use Disorders Initiative and founded the Bridge Clinic at Massachusetts General Hospital, where patients could walk in and be seen by trained experts certified in addiction treatment. I arranged to go out there and see how it worked and met some of the most kind, elegant doctors I ever encountered, including Dr. Laura Kehoe, the clinical director. Patients were accepted at the Bridge Clinic whether or not they had insurance or payment of any kind—nobody was turned away. It also didn't matter if their home was an apartment, a shelter, or an alley—they were still seen. These doctors understood the hard life of addiction in the patients they treated. Dr. Kehoe knew the language, pitfalls, and schemes some still resorted to when interacting with the medical world. All the patients were still treated with dignity, and all they had to do was *cooperate* with the care plans. I knew that Dr. Kehoe had the expertise, kindness, and warmth that Macky needed. She would have saved his life.

* * *

Anne and I had first started to cope with our pain by buying food and feminine hygiene things like soap, shampoo, and personal care products for a homeless shelter and made regular trips there. We bought mountains of warm clothes at a Goodwill and got them cleaned, sorted, and put on hangers by a college student, and we delivered those, too. We both felt good to provide kindness to people who were down and out, usually because of addiction, because we hoped they would feel valued and worthy of understanding. Any one of them could have been Macky, and maybe there was a time he stayed there. We knew that most of the people we tried to help were alienated from family and suffered from either addiction or mental illness, and we found solace in offering them some comfort as they tried to find their way home.

Anne did something more, though. She learned that a state legislator, Alice Peisch, was going to receive constituents nearby to listen to local concerns. Anne went to the meeting and shared Macky's story and how things could have been different if effective help had been available. The aide she met with had also lost a family member to overdose and cared about Anne's message. The recommendations were carried to the Massachusetts legislature, which later created sweeping new legislation called the Massachusetts Opioid Bill. It was ultimately signed into law by the governor the following year, and he described it as a "blueprint for the nation." Anne's efforts were only one small part of how that bill was enacted, but before it was voted on she and I were invited to the statehouse to review the entire draft and recommend changes we thought were needed.

* * *

Meanwhile, I continued to work in hospice and provided inpatient care to terminally ill patients with severe symptoms at a facility in Haverhill, Massachusetts. I have always had profound respect and appreciation for the staff who care for these patients and was proud to be working with them. They knew what had happened to Macky and were especially kind and caring to me.

All of the hospice staff there listened to me talk about what happened and how Macky's death might have been prevented. One of the nurses, Bria Grady, told me she had an idea about how things could change to help other people with addiction.

"Dr. Baker, maybe I can help," she said. "My sister Lori just got elected to Congress and will be sworn in next month. Do you want to talk with her? I know she would care."

Her sister was Lori Trahan, who had recently been elected to the U.S. House of Representatives. She called me, and we talked for more than an hour. She listened to the whole story and then asked what she could do to make things better. We spoke in person during events in her district, and she connected me with her staff who would be drafting legislation.

Lori was sworn into office in January 2019, and she asked me to come to the Capitol and address members of Congress in committee about Macky's story and share what I thought Congress could do. Lori took me to meet Congressman David Trone, who had lost a nephew to overdose at twenty-three, the same age Macky was. Representative Trone promised to work for better care.

Within a few months, Lori and her staff wrote a comprehensive bill called the MATE Act. which would *require* every clinician in the United States with a Drug Enforcement Administration license to learn the basics of addiction and its treatment—the only exception would be physicians who formally trained in addiction medicine. The law that Lori wrote limited that education to a minimum of eight hours of training so that clinicians would not be overburdened.

Together with leadership of the American Society of Addiction Medicine, I met with several members of Congress. One who stood out was Representative Earl "Buddy" Carter from Georgia, a strong Republican leader with different political perspectives from the Democratic sponsors of Lori's bill, but I saw him put politics aside that day.

"You know what, Dr. Baker?" he said. "I'm going to support this bill because it's the right thing to do. I want to help." He signed on as a cosponsor.

Congressional legislation tends to move very slowly, but Lori would not give up and eventually the MATE Act was passed in the House of Representatives by an overwhelming majority and then moved to the Senate for consideration.

* * *

Around the same time I started working with Representative Trahan, some of Macky's writings surfaced. Anne was cleaning his room because I couldn't bring myself to change anything in there, but she still kept it tidy. She came upon some papers he wrote and showed them to me. I didn't want to look at them at first but then realized I felt close to him when I read his words. His fingerprints were smudged on some of the pages and I could still smell the pencil he used to scribble on the paper.

Anne also found items he had left in a basement closet, including "Macky's Book of Art and Writing," written and illustrated by him in 2005, when he was twelve. It contained a variety of innocent stories and drawings that revealed his personality at that age.

Behind a dining room cabinet, she found that poster he made in 2007 titled "The Timeline of My Life." He had glued pictures along the timeline to go along with events that were important to him, and the last one is of him and me together. In the faded photograph, he was missing a front tooth because Homer had accidentally knocked it out. The caption to that one reads, "2005—my Dad goes into Palliative Care!"

I decided to look for more and found a treasure trove. There were many documents stored in his computer that I couldn't open, but what I was able to read was profoundly important to me.

I had also saved letters we had written to each other over the years as well as letters I wrote to others about my life and about Macky's addiction. There were times when our conversations continued on in my dreams at night, and during those dreams we laughed and talked together, leaving me to wake up happy because I thought he was still alive—we had just been talking a few minutes ago, I thought.

With effort, I was able to construct a timeline of what happened and how each of us felt along the way. I began to understand what led to his addiction and how deeply he wanted to stop. A story was unfolding, and I decided to write what I had learned to share with other families what they needed to understand about addiction. Maybe they could prevent addiction in the first place or help an addicted son or daughter before it was too late.

I started writing but saw that raw emotions and painful memories dominated the pages. I wrote about the sorrow I felt after his death but thought that nobody would learn anything new from reading that. I switched my focus to medical information, but that was boring and hard to decipher. The scientific information was accurate; however, it wouldn't benefit anybody because it was as unreadable as a thick, old-fashioned telephone book. Thousands of pages went into the trash or into boxes that I never opened again. I tried not to be discouraged, but I was.

I had attended author readings by accomplished writers to hear about their lives and sometimes had a chance to speak with them afterward, hoping to have some guidance.

After a presentation by Patti Smith, a poet and author as well as a singer, I walked up to her table and tried to engage her.

"I just have one question," I said.

"Yeah? I just have one answer. Keep writing," she said and then turned her attention to someone else.

Kazuo Ishiguro, who won the Nobel Prize in literature, spoke about how hurt he was when someone he didn't know in Minnesota wrote a negative review of one of his books.

Amy Tan was asked why it took so long for her latest book to come out.

"Because I spent five years writing a different one, hated it, and threw it out. Then I started this one."

I realized it wasn't just me who struggled to put words on a page, so I kept at it and wrote wherever I could—at the medical school library, at the Holden public library, at a friend's empty guesthouse on Nantucket, or curled up like a shrimp with my laptop at home. Most of what I wrote never saw the light of day. Vladimir Nabokov wanted his unfinished works to drift away, burned in a pale fire, and I understood why.

Writing the truth was my first priority. That meant I would not create a situation that held more appeal or add a twist that made the writing easier to accomplish. The only suspense or drama that could occur was what really happened, told as accurately as I could remember and supported by what Macky left behind.

Along the way, I went to Macky's grave and told him how things were going and that one day I would get his story out to help others. I wanted him to know I would not give up, and I still go to see him and update what I am doing.

"It's hard, Macky, but this is what we need to do."

* * *

The MATE Act was passed by the Senate on December 22, 2022. Later that evening, the president signed the bill into law. Effective June 27, 2023, every single prescriber in the United States, whether doctor, nurse practitioner, or pharmacist, was required to complete at least eight hours of training in the basics of addiction and its treatment. The education must be completed to obtain or renew a Drug Enforcement Administration license to prescribe controlled substances like OxyContin or any other opioid medication. The new law is not limited to just one year but is permanent. Congresswoman Trahan, with the support of her colleagues in Congress and approval by the president, permanently changed American medicine.

The MATE Act doesn't compel any doctor to start treating patients with addiction. That decision is up to each individual doctor based on their own confidence and commitment. The purpose of the law is to make sure that all doctors at least *understand* the very basics of addiction as a treatable disorder and begin to recognize addiction in their patients and understand the fears of families that they would lose a loved one to overdose. Some doctors will offer treatment themselves and others will be able to refer to providers who are experts in addiction treatment, but no doctor should ever say, "I don't know anything about addiction."

With far more than a million American families already having buried a son, daughter, sister, or brother as a result of overdose and more than 100,000 more deaths every year, overdose deaths are now more than twice as common as traffic fatalities. New understanding by doctors can change that course. Kelly Corredor of the American Society of Addiction Medicine advocated for the MATE Act by asking lawmakers to compare doctors to airline pilots.

"When doctors prescribe opioids, they also need to learn how to manage addiction, the same way that pilots taking off in commercial jets also need to know how to land them."

* * *

I hope that people who suffer from addiction will learn through these pages that they can recover with the right kind of help. I hope that families will learn that substance use disorder is not a choice and that their loved one is still present even though they may be obscured by the convoluted behaviors that accompany untreated addiction.

Maybe there will be many families living with addiction who will learn from Macky's story and my own. They may recognize that knowledge and compassion are the keys to both prevention and recovery. Maybe there will be just one life saved, but even that one person's survival will make every ounce of effort in writing this book worthwhile. Instead of a tragic death and the aftermath of a nightmare that never ends, that family can cherish the joy of life together for a long time to come.

Acknowledgments

Don Fehr, my literary agent at Trident Media Group, believed in me from the very beginning and guided me through the complex publishing world. My editor, Jonathan Kurtz, saw the importance of this story and trusted me to tell the unvarnished truth. My talented production editor, Nicole Carty, refined and polished the writing.

My colleagues Marley Downing, Shawn Dowen, and Dr. JoAnne Nowak helped me discern what mattered most. Dr. Bernice Burkarth, my boss, covered my shifts and said, "Get 'er done, Jim." My dearest friend Anna Deraney listened to me tell Macky's story almost every day for five years. She told me, "Jim, if you save just one life, this effort will be worth it."

Ms. Phyllis Whitten and her husband Dr. Richard Whitten helped me shape an amorphous set of memories into a cohesive story.

Mikelynn Salthouse, my cherished confidante, took my hand and never let go. She read the manuscript and said, "I'm sorry, Jim, but it's not good enough. You need to rewrite it." So I did.

Rusty Shelton of Zilker Media heard my pitch at Dr. Julie Silver's writers conference at Harvard Medical School. He said, "This is a book that people need. Please write it, Dr. Baker."

My children's enduring love motivated me throughout. Casey and Dan ("Homer") pushed through their own pain and supported me every day. My daughter, Dr. Cuff Baker, told me, "Dad, either write the truth or hide under the bed." My love for Macky led to this endeavor, and his writing is the best in the book.

My wife Anne did the most to bring this project to the finish line. She tolerated years of struggle, never wavered in her support, and helped me survive my grief. I understand why the last words I ever heard Macky say were, "I love you, Anne."